SAP Excellence

Series Editors:
Professor Dr. Dr. h.c. mult. Peter Mertens
Universität Erlangen-Nürnberg

Dr. Peter Zencke
SAP AG, Walldorf

Jörg Thomas Dickersbach

Characteristic Based Planning with mySAP SCM™

Scenarios, Processes, and Functions

With contributions by
A. Forstreuter, C. Fuhlbrügge and T. John

With 174 Figures
and 3 Tables

 Springer

Dr. Jörg Thomas Dickersbach
SAP AG
Postfach 14 61
69185 Walldorf
Germany
E-mail: dickersbach@gmx.de

SAP, SAP SEM, SAP SEM/BA, SAP BW, SAP Logo, R/2, R/3, BAPI, Management Cockpit, mySAP, mySAP.com as well as other products and services of SAP and the correspondent logos are trademarks or registered trademarks of SAP AG in Germany and in several other countries all over the world. All other products mentioned are trademarks or registered trademarks of their respective companies.
EVA® is a registered trademark of Stern Stewart & Co.
HTML and XML are trademarks or registered trademarks of W3C®, World Wide Web Consortium, Massachusetts Institute of Technology.
Oros® and ABC Technologies® are registered trademarks of ABC Technologies, Inc.
Microsoft®, WINDOWS®, NT®, Access®, Excel®, Word®, PowerPoint® and SQL Server® are registered trademarks of Microsoft Corporation.
Powersim® is a registered trademark of Powersim Corporation.

Cataloging-in-Publication Data
Library of Congress Control Number: 2005926344

ISBN 3-540-25781-0 Springer Berlin Heidelberg New York

Springer is a part of Springer Science+Business Media
springeronline.com

© Springer-Verlag Berlin Heidelberg 2005
Printed in Germany

Cover design: Erich Kirchner
Production: Helmut Petri
Printing: Strauss Offsetdruck

SPIN 11422655   Printed on acid-free paper – 42/3153 – 5 4 3 2 1 0

Preface

Characteristics are used in SAP as attributes, e.g. to specify the configuration of products or the properties of batches. In many industries – engineering, automotive, mill, pharmaceutical and foods to name the most typical – supply chain planning has to consider these characteristics. APO offers many different functionalities for planning with characteristics, where each of the functionalities has some prerequisites and incompatibilities. Within the design of an implementation there are multiple determinants for the system configuration, and it is very important to understand the interdependencies and limitations at an early stage of the project. This book offers help and advice for the basic design of the implementation by explaining

- the processes and scenarios (process chains) for planning with characteristics,
- the functionalities for planning with characteristics in APO including their prerequisites and incompatibilities and
- the entities, dependencies and system configuration determinants for planning with characteristics in R/3 and APO

in order to avoid the discovery towards the end of the implementation that some parts just do not work together – and this risk is much higher using characteristics because the interdependencies are much less obvious.

We believe that especially with characteristic based planning (a newly introduced term to subsume the different functionalities for planning with characteristics) it is very important to understand the order flow in detail. Therefore we will focus whenever possible on the scenario and use a functionality oriented approach only for those functions which require an extensive explanation or are used in multiple scenarios.

The focus on the selected scenarios does not imply that these are the only possible ones. But with the understanding of these scenarios and the limitation of the functionalities it will be a lot easier to assess whether a specific design is somewhere near the trodden path or not and which incompatibilities might arise.

For the visualisation of the order flow we are using comparatively many screenshots because the appearance of the objects is different depending on the configuration, and for the practical implementation it is helpful to notice the difference whether the characteristics values of an order in APO are due to variant configuration, descriptive characteristics or batch selection.

This book is clearly not an introduction to R/3 and APO in general. Therefore we assume a fairly good understanding about the basic concepts of these systems – in particular SD on R/3-side and DP, PP/DS and ATP on APO-side. Even without a detailed understanding of all of these modules it is possible to understand the basic messages of the book, but for implementation help other sources have to be found – e.g. Dickersbach 2004. References to the literature have been kept to a minimum, instead OSS notes are referenced. Since the focus of this book lies on the application of the APO and R/3 system and the processes and scenarios which can be modelled with these (and less on general advantages and disadvantages of certain processes), this seemed to me the more helpful way.

This document is based on the releases SCM 4.1 and R/3 4.7. For earlier releases additional constraints apply.

First of all I would like to thank Anton Forstreuter, Christian Fuhlbrügge and Thomas John for their extensive help – from the multiple hints about the correct configuration of the system up to the discussions about the ideas and purposes of the functions, processes and scenarios. Without their contribution this book would not have been possible. Many thanks as well to Stefan Elfner and Dr. Sven Eigemann for their help in the area of the batch selection and to Christoph Jerger, Veronika Schmid-Lutz and Dr. Frank Horlacher for their comments and corrections. Finally I would like to thank Tobias Götz for his generous support of this project.

Jörg Thomas Dickersbach   March 2005

Contents

1 Motivation for Planning with Characteristics

Characteristics are used in SAP to specify and provide additional information to objects as materials, resources, batches or orders. From a planning point of view those characteristics are relevant which describe

- the properties of a configurable product for an order (e.g. the engine and the colour of a car) and
- the properties of a product batch (i.e. inventory that was produced under the same conditions and has the same properties).

In R/3 the sales order-oriented configuration of a product lies in the area of the variant configuration, the batch specific product properties are covered with the batch management. In combination with APO both types of characteristic can be used for planning – and there are different ways how to use APO for demand planning, sales order fulfilment and production. To subsume the different possibilities of planning with characteristic in APO we introduce the term 'characteristic based planning' (CBP).

• *Variant Configuration*

In many industries there is a trend towards mass customisation (Knolmayer/Mertens/Zeier 2002). The variant configuration helps to combine the oppositional requirements for large quantities in logistics and for increasing individualisation on the other hand. Due to increasing competition the number of material variants has been increasing recently (Eversheim 1996).

The motivation to use characteristics to specify resp. to configure a product is to reduce the amount and effort for creating new master data for each combination of the characteristics. Though there are cases where it is possible to cover a few different configurations per product by using a different material master for each configuration, in many cases the number of master data would explode and cause problems in performance, transparency, interactive planning and master data management. The main advantage of using characteristics in this area is to reduce the complexity in order to keep the transparency within the supply chain and to avoid the other problems of huge master data quantities. For example it is usually easier to perform a forecast on attributes than for completely configured products.

Another aspect is the increase in the flexibility compared to the effort of creating a new set of master data (material master, BOM, routing, …) for each new characteristic combination.

Typical industries for variant configuration are engineering and construction where often each machine is different in some aspects, automotive industry where most manufacturers support a configuration of the car, mill products (metal, paper & wood) where customers often have specific requirements regarding size and quality and even high tech and consumer products – e.g. for the configuration of PCs. There are cases where a few hundred characteristics are used per product.

● *Batch Management*

The batch characteristics on the other hand are used to describe the properties of a concrete, existent product which are in most cases only known at the time of the goods receipt from the production. Examples for these properties are the shelf life resp. production date or the quality of the batch. The latter is of considerable significance in cases where the production process contains stochastic elements – i.e. the exact product quality of the individual batch is not predictable.

Typical industries for these are once again the mill industries, chemical and pharma (which have often additional requirements regarding batch pureness and shelf life) and consumer products – most of all foods industries.

Usually either variant configuration or batches are used, but there are cases where both variant configuration and batches are required. An example for this are the mill industries as described in chapter 8.

2 Characteristic Based Planning Overview

2.1 Process Overview

Supply chain processes in general span the areas of demand planning, (sales) order fulfilment, distribution, production and procurement. Collaboration processes might be added both towards customers and towards suppliers. For characteristic based planning (CBP) however we focus on the demand planning, sales order fulfilment and production processes because these are affected the most by planning with characteristics and have usually the biggest significance for the relevant industries (with the exception of consumer goods). Another reason is that distribution and procurement support planning with characteristics only to a rather limited extent.

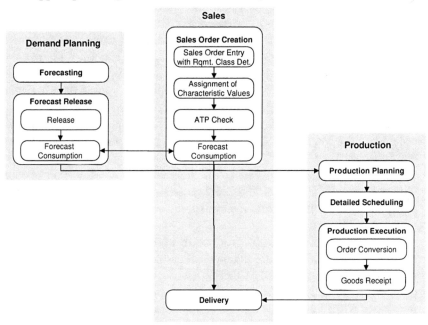

Fig. 2.1. Processes and Process Steps for CBP

Within demand planning, sales and production we define the processes and process steps that are shown in figure 2.1. This is a simplified view because only those elements are shown which are relevant for characteristic based planning – e.g. pricing within the sales order creation process and production order confirmation within the production execution process are left out. Nevertheless it provides a framework for the processes which are considered in the following and their interdependencies. Naturally not all process steps are required for the different cases of supply chain planning with characteristics.

Demand planning has the task to provide the production planning process with forecasts (also named planned independent requirements (PIRs)) to trigger production before the customer places the sales order. If the finished product is configurable, production is only triggered for assembly groups (with the exception of material variants, see chapter 5). The demand for the assembly groups is either forecasted based on the history or calculated from the demand for the finished product. In the latter case demand planning has to be performed on characteristic level. With the forecast release the demand plan becomes relevant for production planning and the forecast consumption is triggered (the forecast is consumed by sales orders).

Sales order creation starts with the entry of the sales item and the (background) determination of the requirements class. The requirements class controls whether make-to-order (usual for variant configuration) or make-to-stock is used. As the next step the characteristic values are assigned to the sales order, either as a configuration (usually interactively) or via batch selection (usually without user interaction). The requested sales item is checked for availability (ATP, available-to-promise) after the characteristic values have been assigned to the sales order. Again a consumption of the forecast is performed. Based on the independent demand of the sales orders and the forecast production planning creates planned orders to cover the demand. To allow the production to start, the planned order must be converted to a production order, which is confirmed after execution and the goods receipt is posted. When the requested product is on stock, the delivery is created and optionally transportation planning towards the customer is performed.

The production starts with production planning. The result of the production planning process are planned orders to cover the requirements. The planned orders are created with the assumption of infinite capacity and component availability. In the subsequent step a feasible plan is created involving a finite scheduling and sequencing of the orders. Experience shows that even with the use of an APS system the two-step approach of an infinite production planning first and a subsequent finite scheduling in a separate step is more adequate. Note 551124 provides additional information on this topic. Depending on the business, before or after the scheduling the planned orders are converted into production orders, production is executed, the production orders are confirmed and goods receipt is posted.

Depending on the scenario the processes might differ significantly. By the scenario we understand the context and the process chain of the company. Some common and typical scenarios are introduced in the following chapter.

The quotation process is not in scope since it is not planning relevant (to provide the information regarding the price and the availability the same functions are used as for the sales order). The impact of characteristics on pricing is not described either since it is entirely within R/3, and APO does not consider prices. Neither in the scope of this book is the financial corporate planning, since the focus is entirely on the SCM related processes.

2.2 Scenarios for Characteristic Based Planning

SCM processes usually have a very wide variance, and the set of functions which are available in APO are combined in many different ways. Many functionalities support characteristics to a certain extent, some functionalities require the use of characteristics and some functionalities do not support characteristics at all. To make things more complicated, the characteristics are embedded in different technical configurations – the classes with their class type in R/3 and the configuration scheme in APO – which bear additional restrictions. Therefore the dependencies between the individual functions and their embedding into the context of the process chain – the scenario – is of crucial importance in order to avoid infeasible implementations.

• *Scenarios*
Under a scenario we understand a typical case for supply chain planning. The scenario is described by a chain of processes which covers either the whole area of the supply chain processes – demand planning, sales and production or at least a significant and typical part of it. Not all of the selected scenarios contain demand planning or production.

Each of the described scenarios is in some industries more common than in others. We have selected seven typical scenarios for characteristic based planning, but these are of course not all possible scenarios. Depending on the specific company requirements it might be appropriate to combine the functionality in a different way to create a new scenario. This combination of functionalities is more complex in the area of characteristics planning than with normal SCM and bears the risk of running into a dead end because of incompatibilities which are not obvious.

Based on the seven selected scenarios it is possible to explain the functionality for characteristic based planning. Most parts of the book relate to one of the seven scenarios, except chapter 3 and 4 about the general properties of characteristics, classes and the configuration scheme and chapter 11 about production planning with characteristics. The reason for the latter is that production planning with characteristics is used similarly throughout most of the scenarios. In the following we will provide an overview about these scenarios.

● *Scenario Overview*
Figure 2.2 provides an overview about the seven selected scenarios regarding their main features in the areas of demand planning, sales and production.

Scenario	Demand Planning	Sales	Production
MTO with Variant Configuration	N.A.	Capable-to-Promise	Production Planning with Characteristics
MTO with Variant Configuration and Planning in Inactive Version	Characteristic Based Forecasting	Multi-Level ATP or Capable-to-Promise	Production Planning with Characteristics
MTO with Variant Configuration and Planning in Active Version	Characteristic Based Forecasting	Forecast Check and/or Allocation Check	Production Planning with Characteristics
Sales from Stock with Characteristics	No Impact	ATP with Characteristics	No Impact
Configure-to-Order with Propagation	N.A.	Capable-to-Promise	PP with Characteristics, Block Planning (optional)
Planning with Shelf Life	No Impact	No Impact	Production Planning with Shelf Life
Sales Order Oriented Planning	Demand Planning	ATP	Production Planning with Order Conversion Rules

Fig. 2.2. Scenario Overview

For the scenario 'configure-to-order with propagation' the option exist to use the block definitions to generate forecasts for the assembly groups (if the assembly groups do not require characteristics for planning). Block planning might be used in other scenarios as well. In the following we describe these scenarios in short.

● *Make-to-Order with Variant Configuration*
The make-to-order scenario with variant configuration is a pure make-to-order scenario which implies that the finished product is not produced

unless there is a sales order for it. In the sales order the configuration of the product – i.e. the characteristic value assignment – is performed per sales order item. Based on the configuration of the sales order the dependent demand for the assembly groups and the capacity requirements for the production are determined via object dependencies.

The configuration might be only for the finished product or for assembly groups as well (multi-level configuration). A special case is the use of material variants which refer to a fix configuration but are not configurable themselves. Since we are in a make-to-order (MTO) environment the ATP check in the sales order uses either

- capable-to-promise (CTP) to create planned orders for the product considering the production capacity and optionally the component availability as well,
- multi-level ATP to create planned orders for the product checking whether the components are available or the
- checking horizon if neither the production capacity nor the component availability are real bottlenecks.

Examples for this scenario are often found in the engineering industry.

● *Make-to-Order with Variant Configuration and Planning*

Make-to-order with variant configuration and demand planning has the advantage that it is possible to plan the demand for the assembly groups based on the demand for the finished product: The required functionality to perform demand planning taking the characteristic values into account is characteristic based forecasting (CBF).

This is performed in two different ways, and for each way we define an own scenario. Based on the demand for the finished product the dependent demand is calculated either in an inactive planning version or in the planning segment of the active version. If the dependent demand is calculated in an inactive planning version, it is transformed into a forecast for the assembly group. For this scenario either the multi-level ATP or the CTP check are the best options. For the scenario with planning in the active version the forecast check is appropriate.

● *Sales from Stock with Characteristics*

Products like electrolytic capacitors, steel assembly groups or pharmaceutical products are produced with a make-to-stock strategy but have properties which do not satisfy all customers. These properties might be connected with the expiry date or due to stochastic production conditions and are stored as batch characteristics. In this case the characteristics of the product have to be considered in the ATP check as well. In this scenario no planning is performed on characteristic level. Another restriction for this scenario is that the ATP check is limited to batches – i.e. no planned receipts are used for confirmation.

• *Configure-to-Order with Propagation*
Configure-to-order with propagation is a very common scenario for the mill industries. This scenario is again a make-to-order scenario, though sometimes without the use of a make-to-stock requirements class. The peculiarity in this process is that assembly groups and key components (steel coils, paper reels, ...) have batch characteristics which are important for planning. Since the mill industries have a divergent material flow, many different finished products will have dependent demands for the key components. These dependent demands might have different requirements for the characteristic values of the batches. Additionally these key components have usually a comparatively long lead time. One main objective in this scenario is therefore usually to check whether the right amount of the key component with the required properties is available. These properties are recorded as the batch valuation.

Differing from the variant configuration not only the finished product is configurable but many assembly levels and the key component have batch characteristics as well. For the finished product both class types for variant configuration and for batches are required.

The sales orders for the finished product has usually a make-to-order strategy, but the assembly groups and the key component are produced as make-to-stock. To create production orders with a valuation in a make-to-stock segment, the IS Mill solution is required on R/3-side. Typically the ATP check for the sales order uses the CTP functionality. If the production of the basic raw material is planned as well or significant set-up is required for the assembly group, block planning is often used. Another feature of this scenario is that the characteristics requirements for the batch selection are usually not discrete values but ranges of values.

• *Planning with Shelf Life*
In some industries as food or pharma the shelf life of the products needs to be considered already during planning. Typically these products are planned as make-to-stock, and the relevant products – often the finished product – have shelf life specific batch characteristics.

For the planning in APO the shelf life uses separate functions, and the product is not relevant for characteristics planning. Characteristics are only required in combination with APO to transfer the shelf life of the batches.

● *Sales Order Oriented Planning*
In many cases neither a pure make-to-stock nor a pure make-to-order strategy is applied for the business. Sales order oriented planning allows to combine advantages of the make-to-stock production as the use of lot-sizes and the consideration of inventories with keeping a reference to the customer: Forecast is consumed on customer resp. customer group level and planned orders are only converted if they are pegged to sales orders.

● *Industry Focus of the Scenarios*
Each of the described scenarios has a main focus on one or more industries. Figure 2.3 shows the industry relevance of these scenarios:

Scenario	Engineering	Automotive	High Tech/ Consumer Electronics	Mill	Chemicals & Pharma	Foods
MTO with Variant Configuration	●	●	●	●		
MTO with Variant Configuration and Planning in Inactive Version	●	●	●			
MTO with Variant Configuration and Planning in Active Version				●		
Sales from Stock with Characteristics			●	●	●	
Configure-to-Order with Propagation				●		
Planning with Shelf Life					●	●
Sales Order Oriented Planning	●		●		●	

Fig. 2.3. Industry Relevance of the Scenarios

In engineering – especially for special purpose machines – as well as in the automotive industry make-to-order with variant configuration is used to large extent. Sometimes make-to-order with variant configuration is used for the consumer goods and the high tech industries as well in more technical consumer goods like PCs. The scenario 'configure-to-order with characteristic propagation' is mostly used in the mill industries, the make-to-order with variant configuration and planning in the active version offers for the mill industries additionally the possibility to plan for the assembly groups. The scenario 'sales from stock with characteristics' is also interesting for the mill industries, but less for processes with production than for the sales of unfinished goods. Other industries for this scenario are industries with perishable products as pharma or industries with stochastic production processes like the high tech industry. The consideration of shelf life already at the planning stage is most important for foods industries but often used for pharmaceutical companies as well. Sales order oriented planning finally might be used by any industry which is neither a pure make-to-stock nor a pure make-to-order production.

2.3 System Configuration Determinants

There are some basic settings for the configuration of the scenarios which are rather fundamental in the sense that it is difficult to change them without major re-design or re-implementation. These four determinants are

- the **requirements strategy**: Here only the account assignment is of importance, i.e. whether a make-to-stock or a make-to-order strategy is applied.
- the **class type**: Characteristics are combined in classes. The classes have class types which limit their usage.
- the **configuration scheme**: in APO two different configuration schemes exist, the VC (variant configuration)-configuration scheme and the CDP (characteristic dependent planning)-configuration scheme.
- the **master data object**: In APO 4.1 there are two alternative master data objects for production planning, the production process model (PPM) and the production data structure (PDS).

For these determinants a short explanation is given in the following.

● *Requirements Strategy*

One main differentiator from a business point of view is the production strategy (make-to-order vs. make-to-stock). The decision whether make-to-order or make-to-stock is used in combination has implications not only towards SCM. Other affected processes are billing, warehousing and delivery.

Usually make-to-order is used to keep the link between the customer and the configured or valuated product via customer order specific planning segments and assignments. If configured or valuated products are used within a make-to-stock scenario, it has to be ensured that the topics mentioned above are either no issues for the specific case or are taken care of in a different way. Technically the decision whether a scenario is make-to-stock or make-to-order is based on the account assignment in the requirements class as defined in the R/3-customising, figure 2.4.

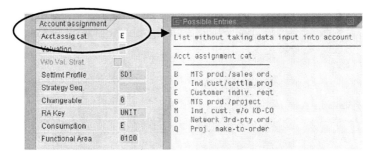

Fig. 2.4. Requirements Class

For a make-to-stock scenario the account assignment category is usually blank. The make-to-order strategy is common for the use of variant configuration and necessary in combination with the VC-configuration scheme. Make-to-stock is used for the sales from stock scenario and the shelf life scenario.

• *Class Type*
The class type is a technical setting in the class which controls its usage for certain functions and processes. The class type is described in more detail in chapter 3.

• *Configuration Scheme*
The configuration scheme is a technical setting in APO which controls the modelling of the characteristics for planning. In short the VC-configuration scheme allows a configuration only for sales orders, and the CDP-configuration scheme allows a configuration for other objects like forecast, planned orders, production orders and batches as well. The significance of the configuration scheme is described in detail in chapter 4. The choice of the configuration scheme is made on client level.

• *Master Data*
The PPM is the master data which was available from the very beginning of APO but will not be developed any further due to some structural limitations (mainly the lack of engineering change management). The alternative to the PPM is the PDS. The functionality of the PDS was increased for APO 4.1. In the releases APO 3.1 and 4.0 the PDS was called run-time object (RTO). The SAP recommendation is to use PDS for new implementations whenever possible.

• *System Configuration Determinants for the Selected Scenarios*

Figure 2.5 provides an overview about the configuration determinants for the selected scenarios:

	Strategy		Class Type		Config. Scheme		Master Data	
	MTO	MTS	300	023	VC	CDP	PDS	PPM
MTO with Variant Configuration	X	--- *	X		X	(x)	X	---
MTO with Variant Configuration and Planning in Inactive Version	X	--- *	X		X	(x)	X	---
MTO with Variant Configuration and Planning in Active Version	X	(x)	X		---	X	X	---
Sales from Stock with Characteristics	---	X		X	---	X		
Configure-to-Order with Propagation Requires IS Mill!	X	(x)	X	X		X	X	X
Planning with Shelf Life	--- **	X			X	X		
Sales Order Oriented Planning	(x)	X						

| X | Supported / Required | (x) | Possible but Unusual | | Indifferent / Not Required | --- | Not Compatible |

* Possible in Combination with the CDP-Configuration Scheme but Not Recommended
** Technically Possible but Not Compatible from a Business Point of View

Fig. 2.5. Configuration Determinants for the Selected Scenarios

Though it is technically possible to perform the configuration of the sales order in combination with a make-to-stock strategy and the VC-configuration scheme, the correct assignment of the receipts to the demands is not ensured any more. Variant configuration as a functionality might be used in the combination of CDP-configuration relevance and macros with the PPM as well, but our definition of the variant configuration scenario includes the transfer of object dependencies from R/3. This is not possible with the PPM.

Shelf life planning does not require any configuration on product level and is therefore independent of the configuration scheme. It is however not possible to combine the shelf life planning functionality with a VC-configuration relevance (e.g. resulting from variant configuration).

As figure 2.5 shows there are quite some incompatibilities. If the switches for the implementation are set wrongly – especially the configuration scheme in APO – this will result in significant additional work to correct this.

2.4 Functions for Characteristic Based Planning in APO

Within the five APO modules DP, SNP, PP/DS, ATP and TP/VS many functions exist which support characteristics or do not support characteristics. Some of these are even incompatible with characteristics – i.e. if characteristics are used, the function does not work – others merely ignore the characteristics. Then there are some functions which require characteristics. Additionally there are some cross-module functions for which the same applies. Figure 2.6 provides an overview about the most common functions and how they relate to planning with characteristics.

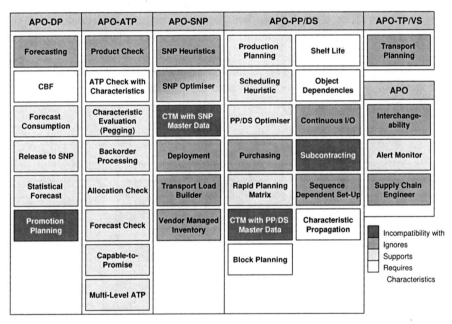

APO-DP	APO-ATP	APO-SNP	APO-PP/DS		APO-TP/VS
Forecasting	Product Check	SNP Heuristics	Production Planning	Shelf Life	Transport Planning
CBF	ATP Check with Characteristics	SNP Optimiser	Scheduling Heuristic	Object Dependencies	APO
Forecast Consumption	Characteristic Evaluation (Pegging)	CTM with SNP Master Data	PP/DS Optimiser	Continuous I/O	Interchange-ability
Release to SNP	Backorder Processing	Deployment	Purchasing	Subcontracting	Alert Monitor
Statistical Forecast	Allocation Check	Transport Load Builder	Rapid Planning Matrix	Sequence Dependent Set-Up	Supply Chain Engineer
Promotion Planning	Forecast Check	Vendor Managed Inventory	CTM with PP/DS Master Data	Characteristic Propagation	
	Capable-to-Promise		Block Planning		
	Multi-Level ATP				

■ Incompatibility with
▨ Ignores
▥ Supports
☐ Requires

Characteristics

Fig. 2.6. Overview about APO Functions and CBP

Most of the CBP relevant functionality is within the module PP/DS, but DP and ATP do offer some functions as well. SNP does not support CBP with a small exception for the SNP optimiser and shelf life. TP/VS does not support characteristics at all nor does it have any relevance for its planning tasks.

CTM does neither support the VC- nor CDP-configuration scheme – if the PDS or PPM contains object dependencies resp. characteristic propagation, the CTM run terminates with an error. An exception is the use of material variants for CTM with PP/DS master data, where the object dependencies are exploded for the PDS before their integration with APO.

Descriptive characteristics on the other hand can be used for demand prioritisation.

The ATP check with characteristics is only possible with the CDP-configuration scheme. Multi-level ATP and the rapid planning matrix are only compatible for the VC-configuration scheme. With 'characteristic propagation' we understand the function of the PPM to propagate a valuation of the output product to the input product (though the propagation is possible with the PDS as well, with this function we refer only to the PPM). Block planning does not necessarily require an integration of characteristics from R/3 to APO but can be used with a simple classification of the routing as well. Sequence dependent set-up is independent of any characteristics values, though reference characteristics can be applied to set the set-up group depending on characteristic values as explained in chapter 11.

• *System Configuration Determinants for the Planning Functions*
Figure 2.7 provides an overview about the prerequisites for the functionalities that require characteristics.

	Strategy		Class Type		Config. Scheme		Master Data	
	MTO	MTS	300	023	VC	CDP	PDS	PPM
Characteristic Based Forecasting	X	(x)	X		X	X		
Multi-Level ATP	X	X	X		X	---		
ATP on Characteristic Level	---	X	(x)	X	---	X		
Block Planning			(x)		X	X	X	X
Integration of Object Dependencies	X	(x)	X		X	X	X	---
Characteristic Propagation in the PPM			X	(x)	---	X	---	X
Shelf Life	(x)	X		X				
Rapid Planning Matrix	X	---	(x)		X	---	X	---

| X | Supported / Required   (x) | Possible but Unusual | Indifferent / Not Required   --- | Not Compatible |

Fig. 2.7. System Configuration Determinants for Functions

For the mill industries it might be desired to perform ATP on characteristic level including planned receipts (it is only with IS Mill possible to integrate valuated planned receipts in the make-to-stock segment with R/3). In this case the class type 300 is necessary to valuate the receipts. Note that rules based ATP with characteristic substitution is not released for variant configuration (i.e. it is only released if just batches are checked – as described in the scenario 'sales from stock with characteristics'). Block planning can be performed with a fix classification of the activities. In this case no integration of classes is required. In most cases configuration is used however. For the mill industries sometimes it is required to use variant

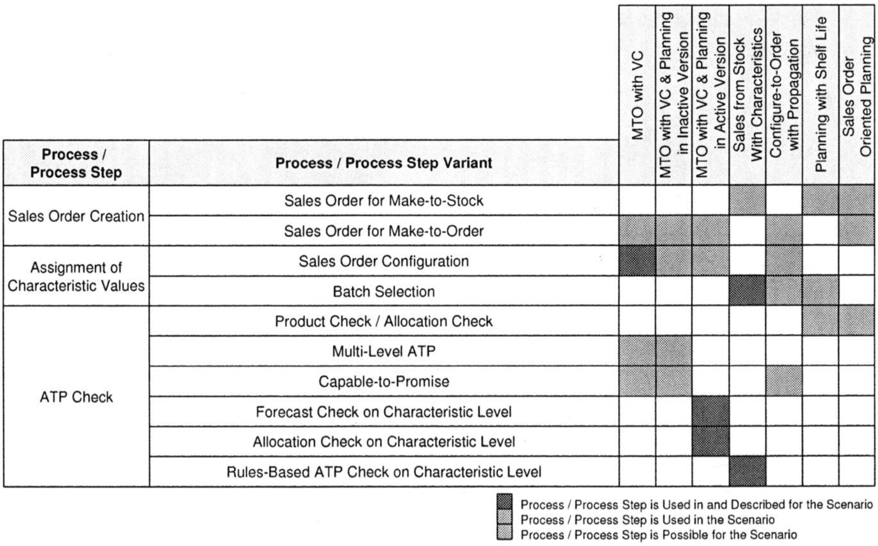

Process / Process Step	Process / Process Step Variant	MTO with VC	MTO with VC & Planning in Inactive Version	MTO with VC & Planning in Active Version	Sales from Stock With Characteristics	Configure-to-Order with Propagation	Planning with Shelf Life	Sales Order Oriented Planning
Sales Order Creation	Sales Order for Make-to-Stock				■		■	■
	Sales Order for Make-to-Order	■	■	■		■		■
Assignment of Characteristic Values	Sales Order Configuration	■	■	■		■		
	Batch Selection				■	■	■	
ATP Check	Product Check / Allocation Check					■	■	■
	Multi-Level ATP	■	■	■		■		
	Capable-to-Promise	■	■	■		■		
	Forecast Check on Characteristic Level			■				
	Allocation Check on Characteristic Level			■				
	Rules-Based ATP Check on Characteristic Level			■				

■ Process / Process Step is Used in and Described for the Scenario
■ Process / Process Step is Used in the Scenario
□ Process / Process Step is Possible for the Scenario

Fig. 2.9. Process Step Variants for Sales

For the **ATP check** almost the whole range of functionalities is used for the different scenarios – though only a few alternatives are recommended per scenario. Figure 2.9 shows the process variants for sales. Depending on the representation of the forecast (see process step 'forecast release') the forecast check considers the characteristic values as well. The ATP check on characteristic level does not necessarily require rules-based ATP, but in most cases the option for a characteristic substitution is desired.

• *Production Process Step Variants*
The main processes for production are production planning (i.e. the process of creating the planned orders), detailed scheduling, production execution with the conversion and processing of the production order and goods receipt. Depending on the configuration relevance and the master data (PDS or PPM), different possibilities exist for **production planning** to use either object dependencies or characteristic propagation in the PPM to control the selection of the components and the capacity requirements of the planned orders. If block planning is used, the planned orders are scheduled into the matching blocks. **Detailed scheduling** offers the two functions of scheduling heuristics or the PP/DS optimiser. The **planned order conversion** is done automatically with the transfer to R/3 if the CDP-configuration relevance is used. With the use of conversion rules it can be ensured that planned orders are only converted if sales orders exist for

them. **Goods receipt** finally may require a batch valuation if batch characteristics are used. Figure 2.10 shows the process variants for production.

Process / Process Step	Process / Process Step Variant	MTO with VC	MTO with VC & Planning in Inactive Version	MTO with VC & Planning in Active Version	Sales from Stock With Characteristics	Configure-to-Order with Propagation	Planning with Shelf Life	Sales Order Oriented Planning
Production Planning	Production Planning (without Characteristics)				X			X
	Production Planning with VC-Characteristics	X						
	Production Planning with CDP-Characteristics	X	X	X		X		
	Block Planning					X		
	Production Planning with Shelf Life						X	
Detailed Scheduling	Scheduling Heuristics	X				X		
	PP/DS Optimisation	X				X		
Order Conversion	Order Conversion	X				X		
	Order Conversion with Conversion Rule							X
Goods Receipt	Goods Receipt	X				X		X
	Goods Receipt with Batch Characteristics				X	X	X	X

Process / Process Step is Used in and Described for the Scenario
Process / Process Step is Used in the Scenario
Process / Process Step is Possible for the Scenario

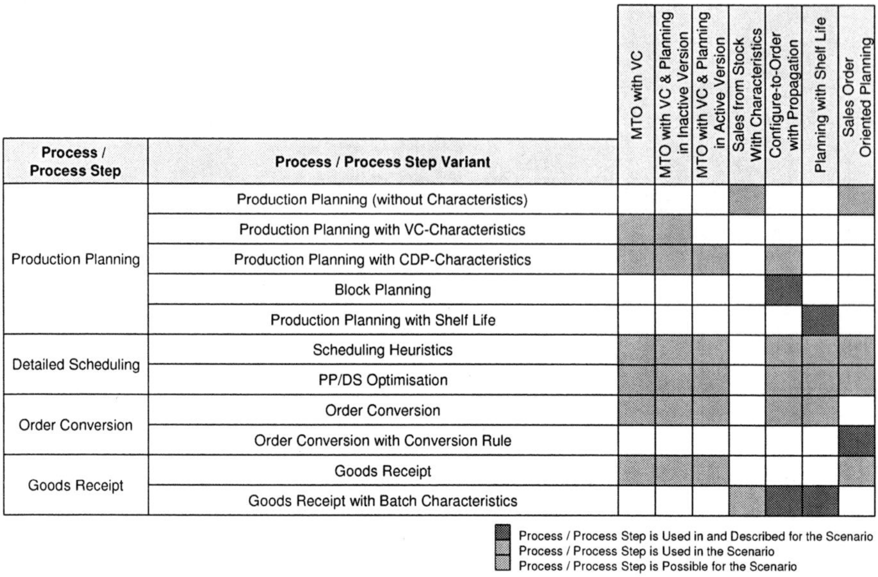

Fig. 2.10. Process Step Variants for Production

Specific for CBP is the consideration of object dependencies and characteristic propagation in production planning. Block planning covers different aspects which are all CBP relevant and has an impact on production planning as well.

3 Characteristics and Classes

3.1 Characteristics and Classes in R/3

Characteristics allow to attach attributes to a material, a routing, a work center, a batch or an order. These attributes are used for different purposes, and only some of them are relevant for characteristic based planning (CBP). For example the usage of material characteristics to search for materials by their technical properties is rather targeted for production engineering, and the usage of work center characteristics to define resource alternatives for APO is not relevant for characteristics based planning either. For CBP we focus on characteristics that are used to describe the configuration of a product in the sales order and characteristics that describe the planning relevant properties of batches. Note 714929 provides additional information about the properties of characteristics in combination with planning in APO.

• *Overview*

Characteristics must be assigned to a class in order to use them in any SAP application. The usage of the characteristics is defined by the class type, though the same characteristic can be assigned to different classes of different class types. Figure 3.1 sketches this interdependency.

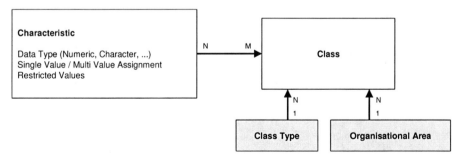

Fig. 3.1. Characteristics and Classes

Characteristics and classes are master data both in R/3 and in APO.

• *Characteristics*
The characteristics are created with transaction CT04 (both in R/3 and in APO) and contain the information about the data type, whether single or multiple values can be assigned and whether the values for the characteristic are restricted or not (checkbox 'additional values' on the values-view). Supported data types are character, numeric, date and time.

• *Classes*
Classes are created with transaction CL02 (both in R/3 and in APO). The key for the class is its name and its type, therefore the same class name can be used for different class types. Each class has a class type which restricts its usage. Table 3.1 lists the most important class types on R/3-side for characteristic based planning in APO and their usage.

Table 3.1. Class Types in R/3 and their Usage

Class Type	Usage	Assignment
018	Task List	Routing
019	Work Center	Work Center
023	Batch Classification	Material Master
200	Material Classification	Material Master
300	Variant Configuration	Material Master

For characteristics based planning only the class types 023 for batches and 300 for variant configuration are relevant. The class types 018 and 019 are used only in R/3 to valuate the master data. This information is used in the integration to APO either for block planning (class type 018, see chapter 8.3) or for the transfer of alternative resources (class type 019, see Dickersbach 2004). The material class for configurable products (class type 200) is used for a special case within the variant configuration scenario (see chapter 5).

• *Organisational Areas*
For the integration of classes and characteristics to APO the organisational area is used as the filter criterion. The assignment of the organisational area to the class is optional for most usages in R/3 but helpful to distinguish those characteristics which are used for planning in APO and those which are only relevant for R/3. The customising for the organisational area is done with the path

    Cross-Application Components → Classification System → Classes → Maintain Object Types and Class Types.

or with the transaction O1CL (in R/3 and in APO). Though the assignment of the organisational area to the classes and the characteristics is transferred to APO, the transfer of the organisational area itself is not integrated and must therefore be created in APO as well.

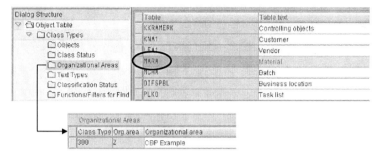

Fig. 3.2. Organisational Areas (R/3 and APO)

The class type for material (table MARA) has to be selected before choosing the organisational area. The organisational area is class type specific. The assignment of both the class and the characteristics to the organisational area takes place in the class.

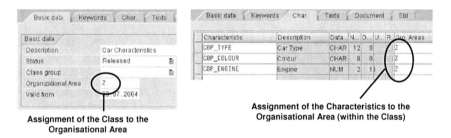

Fig. 3.3. Assignment of the Class and the Characteristics to the Org. Area (R/3 and APO)

• *Assignment of Classes to the Master Data*

The assignment of the classes to the material master is done in the 'classification'-view. Only classes of one class type are displayed, but with F7 it is possible to switch between the class types. For variant configuration (class type 300) multiple classes can be assigned, for batch classification (class type 023) only one class is allowed. With the transaction CL24N it is possible to provide an overview about the class assignment to the material master and perform additional assignments as shown in figure 3.4.

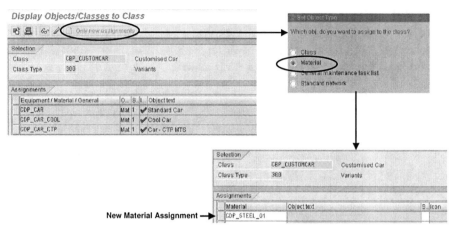

Fig. 3.4. Class Assignment Overview

Within the routing the classification is maintained from the operation via the menu path *Extras → Classification → Operation* and for the work center with the menu path *Extras → Classification*.

3.2 Transfer of Characteristics and Classes to APO

The transfer of classes and characteristics to APO is done via the CIF, and the organisational area is used as the selection criterion. For the transfer of classes and characteristics a separate integration model should be used (see note 714929), and the characteristics and classes should be transferred before the materials are transferred.

• *Class Type Correspondence*
From a planning point of view only the R/3-class types 023 for batch classification and 300 for variant configuration are relevant. The class type 300 has its correspondence on APO side with the same class type. Since planning with the CDP-configuration scheme is based on the APO-class type 400, a R/3-class with type 300 is transferred as a class of the type 300 and additionally (if the CDP-configuration scheme is active) as a class with type 400.

For the use of batch classification the R/3-class type 023 is transferred as APO-class type 400 and additionally as class type 230, figure 3.5.

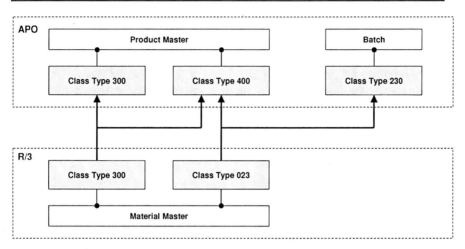

Fig. 3.5. Class Types in R/3 and in APO

The class type 230 is used in APO only for the valuation of the batches and is not assigned to the product master.

• *Assignment to the Product Master*

The assignment of the class to the product master is done automatically during CIF-transfer. The class is only assigned to the product master if the class contains characteristics. The class assignment can only be displayed in APO but not changed. Figure 3.6 shows how to display the class assignment for further classes (if more than one class is assigned to the product).

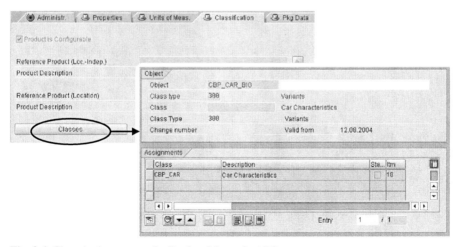

Fig. 3.6. Class Assignment to the Product Master in APO

● *Transfer of Batches*

If batch classification is used in R/3 for CDP-configuration relevant products, the integration of batches is required. The transfer of batches has to be selected explicitly in the CIF-model. The transfer of stocks is not sufficient to integrate the batches with their characteristic values with APO.

4 Configuration Scheme in APO

For historical reasons there are two types of configuration schemes (formerly known as class systems) in APO: Variant configuration (VC) and characteristic dependent planning (CDP). The VC-configuration scheme was developed mainly for the automotive and engineering industries and is closely linked to the variant configuration in R/3, whereas the CDP-configuration scheme was developed mainly for the mill industries. The main difference is that with the VC-configuration scheme only the sales orders have a configuration (i.e. characteristics with values). Other objects (e.g. planned orders) do not have an own configuration but a reference to the sales order via an internal key. Therefore the configuration that is displayed for a planned order is the configuration of the sales order. The complete configuration – even for multiple levels – is defined at the entry of the sales order. Since only the sales order has a configuration, the make-to-order strategy is mandatory to keep the link between the sales order and the receipts during planning.

With the CDP-configuration scheme sales orders, forecasts, planned orders, production orders and batches have an own configuration. Another difference is that the CDP-configuration scheme allows demands (sales orders, dependent demands) to define requirements for the characteristic values of their supplies. Chapter 11.1.2 describes the logic for planning with the CDP-configuration scheme in detail. When using the CDP-configuration scheme, the characteristics values are considered in pegging. Therefore only few characteristics should be used. Note 526883 provides additional information about the implications of using too many characteristics for CDP.

Both configuration schemes offer advantages but in SCM 4.1 it is still only possible to use either the VC-configuration scheme or the CDP-configuration scheme per client. The customising path to define which configuration scheme is active for the client is

    APO → Basis Settings → Define Configuration Relevance.

● *Configuration Scheme and Configuration Relevance*
The term 'configuration scheme' refers to the setting of in the customising, whereas the 'configuration relevance' denotes whether the product actually

uses characteristics for planning. With APO 4.1 a product has either the configuration relevance as defined in the customising or none (e.g. when planning with shelf life). The outlook for further releases is to define the configuration relevance on product level (as a possibility).

● *Configuration Schemes and Functions*

Since APO 3.1 an effort has been started to harmonise the configuration schemes. Starting with the characteristic and class master data in APO 3.1, the product master was harmonised in APO 4.0 and the transactional data in APO 4.1. The latter two have been mostly internal changes, but with the result that more functions can be used with both configuration schemes. Table 4.1 provides an overview about the supported functions.

Table 4.1. Configuration Scheme and Functions

Function	VC-Configuration Scheme	CDP-Configuration Scheme
Characteristic Based Forecasting	Yes	Yes
Variant Configuration	Yes	Yes
Multi-Level Variant Configuration	Yes	No
Batch Selection	No	Yes
Multi-Level ATP	Yes	No
ATP with Characteristics	No	Yes
Characteristic Values in Pegging	No	Yes
Object Dependencies in the PDS	Yes	Yes
Characteristic Propagation in the PPM	No	Yes
Block Planning	Yes	Yes
Shelf Life[1]	Yes	Yes
Planned Order Transfer	Yes	Automatic Conversion

[1] Shelf Life Functionality is Independent of the Configuration Scheme

For shelf life the product does not need any configuration relevance. Characteristics are only required for the batches, therefore the configuration scheme does not have any impact on the shelf life functionality. It is however not possible to use shelf life for products with VC-configuration relevance. A CDP-configuration relevance on the other hand does not interfere with the shelf life functionality.

5 Make-to-Order with Variant Configuration

5.1 Scenario Description

5.1.1 Process Chain

In some industries – e.g. in engineering – the finished products are configurable (often up to a few hundred characteristics) and the number of units sold per product and characteristic combination is far from a commodity. In these cases the product is only produced after it is sold – i.e. after the sales order has been entered. The configuration for the product is maintained in the sales order.

The make-to-order strategy implies that the ATP check does not need to look for the availability of the finished product. The typical ATP method for this scenario is capable-to-promise (CTP) where planned orders are created for the product – if required, for several BOM levels including capacity check and purchase requisitions.

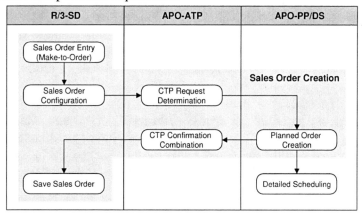

Fig. 5.1. Process Chain for Make-to-Order with Variant Configuration

The focus for this scenario is on the sales side – there is no demand planning, and few specifics for production planning and scheduling. Figure 5.1 shows the process flow for the sales order creation.

For this scenario we assume that object dependencies are used and have to be integrated with APO.

• Sales Order Creation and Assignment of Characteristic Values
The process starts with the entry of a sales order. The sales order is created and configured as described in chapter 5.2.

• ATP Check
Since we are in a make-to-order scenario the finished product will not be available. There are three sensible options to perform an ATP check nevertheless, of which capable-to-promise (CTP) is the most common.

• Capable-to-Promise
During the CTP-check a planned order is created and checked for capacity. The capacity check is either on a time-continuous and sequence dependent basis or based on a bucket capacity. The latter is available with APO 4.1 and the recommended alternative. The CTP-check can be applied for several levels, though with each level and with each finite resource the complexity increases. It is strongly recommended to keep the capacity check as simple as possible. Missing components might either be produced resp. procured or regarded as a constraint. This is controlled by the planning procedure of the product. This way both the production capacity and the material availability are checked. The object dependencies are considered as well. The assumption for this alternative is that both the production capacity and the material availability might be bottlenecks. The use of CTP has major impacts and restrictions for production planning (especially if time-continuous CTP is used). For a more detailed description of the properties and risks of CTP see note 426563 and Dickersbach (2004).

• Multi-Level ATP
Another option is the use of the multi-level ATP check. This option requires however that the key components are already available. Instead of the finished product the components for the finished product are checked (if required, for several levels). The demand for the components is calculated using the PDS (the PPM could be used for multi-level ATP as well, but is not recommended for this scenario), and both the planned order duration and the object dependencies are considered. The assumption is that the production capacity is no bottleneck and that the components are

planned for. The use of multi-level ATP has impacts and restrictions for production planning. A limitation for the use of multi-level ATP is that the CDP-configuration scheme is not supported. A more detailed explanation of the multi-level ATP is provided in Dickersbach (2004). If planning of the assembly groups has a significant role within the business, the scenario 'make-to-order with variant configuration and planning in an inactive version' should be considered, therefore we do not assume the use of multi-level ATP for this scenario.

• Checking Horizon
The third option is the ATP check using the checking horizon. The sales order will be confirmed outside the checking horizon which represents the required lead time to produce the product. This setting is product specific and does not take the actual production capacity or the actual component availability into account. The assumption is that the check horizon provides a sufficient time buffer to avoid material or capacity shortages. In most cases this leads either to unnecessarily late confirmations or causes problems in production and/or non-deliveries. With APO the two other methods provide usually better results, and therefore this option is not explained any further.

• Production Planning and Detailed Scheduling
Production planning is done by the CTP check, but a detailed scheduling step still needs to be performed.

5.1.2 System Configuration Determinants

The prerequisites for this scenario are the use of make-to-order assignments, class type 300 and the PDS master data object. The object dependencies are transferred from R/3 and used for production planning in APO. Both the VC- and the CDP-configuration scheme are able to support this scenario, though it is rather unusual to use the CDP-configuration scheme. The exception are the mill industries.

Requirements Class Account Assignment	Class Type (R/3)	Configuration Scheme	Master Data
Make-to-Stock	Batch (023)	CDP	PPM
Make-to-Order	Variant Config. (300)	VC	PDS

Required / Supported
Supported but Unusual
Not Supported

Fig. 5.2. System Configuration Determinants for MTO with Variant Configuration

If the CDP-configuration scheme is used, the planned orders are converted into production orders when they are transferred to R/3. Therefore the option to transfer only production orders (i.e. planned orders with the conversion indicator) should be evaluated in this case. Another downside is the performance criticality of planning with many CDP-characteristics.

The usage of a make-to-stock strategy in combination with the CDP-configuration scheme would be technically possible, though it is not appropriate for this scenario and the industries in target (engineering and automotive). This option will be mentioned as a special case within the scenario 'configure-to-order with propagation' in chapter 8.

The make-to-order scenario with variant configuration requires the use of the PDS master data because it is not possible to integrate the object dependencies with the PPM. Though it would be possible to use a PPM in combination with the CDP-configuration scheme and model the object dependencies as macros in APO, this is a very circumstantial way. We define the integration of the object dependencies from R/3 as a part of the scenario, and therefore the PPM is incompatible with this scenario.

5.1.3 Configurable Material

The standard material type for configurable materials is not the 'finished product' FERT but the 'configurable material' KMAT. This includes among others that an appropriate item category group (see chapter 5.2) is set and that the checkbox for variant configuration is set on the 'basic data 2'-view, figure 5.3.

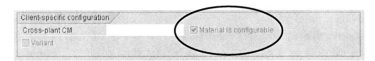

Fig. 5.3. Checkbox 'Material is Configurable' (R/3)

5.1.4 Configuration Profile

For the use of the variant configuration functionality in R/3 a configuration profile is required which defines the class types and the organisational areas that are allowed for a material. The configuration profile is maintained with the transaction CU41.

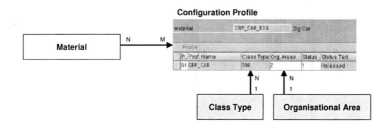

Fig. 5.4. Configuration Profile (R/3)

Only the class types 300 and 001 are allowed for the configuration profile. For a multi-level configuration and the configuration via material class additional settings in the detail of the configuration profile are necessary as described in the chapters 5.4 and 5.5.

5.2 Variant Configuration in the Sales Order

The configuration of a product is performed as an assignment of characteristic values to the sales order.

• *Requirements Class and Item Category Group*
Prerequisites for the usage of the variant configuration functionality in the sales order are that the requirements class and item category support the variant configuration. Within the requirements class the indicator for configuration has at least to allow configuration.

The standard item category for configuration is TAC. The item category is determined via the sales order type and the item category group as shown in figure 5.6. The customising paths for these entities are

  Sales and Distribution → Sales → Sales Documents → Sales Document Item → Define Item Categories

resp. *Define Item Category Groups* and *Assign Item Categories*.

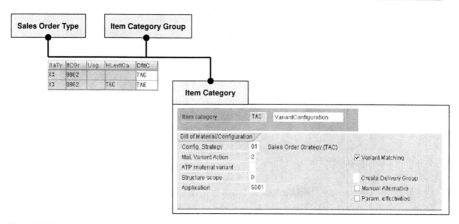

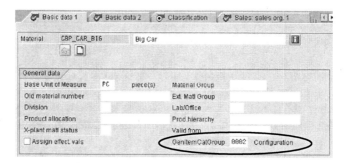

Fig. 5.5. Item Category for Variant Configuration (R/3)

The standard item category group for configuration is 0002 and is maintained in the 'basic data 1' and the 'sales org. 2' views of the material master as shown in figure 5.6.

Fig. 5.6. Assignment of the Item Category Group to the Material Master (R/3)

For the material type KMAT (configurable material) the item category group 0002 is set by default.

• *Configuration of the Sales Order*
The configuration of the sales order is performed in a follow-up screen after the sales order item has been entered as shown in figure 5.7.

.

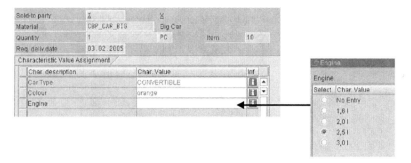

Fig. 5.7. Configuration of the Sales Order (R/3)

Depending on the configuration of the characteristics (i.e. whether the flag for additional values is set), the values are selected from the list or entered freely. It is possible to restrict the characteristic value combinations using variant tables. The assignment of the characteristic values is done before the ATP check is carried out. Not all characteristics have to be specified. Generally the use of unspecified characteristics is not recommended if the CDP-configuration scheme is used due to problems in pegging, production planning and ATP on characteristic level (see chapter 11.1). Since the variant configuration scenario is usually performed with a make-to-order strategy, the use of the sales order segment solves these problems.

● *Sales Order Representation in APO*
The sales order is transferred to APO with its configuration. In the product view (transaction /SAPAPO/RRP3) the green triangle indicates that a valuation exists. For the VC-configuration scheme in APO the order and the configuration details are shown in figure 5.8. The window on the left side shows the sales order segments.

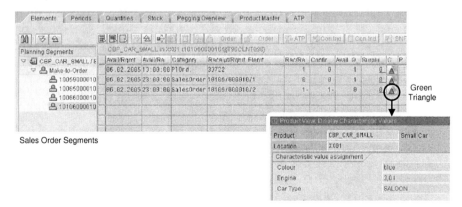

Fig. 5.8. Sales Order with VC-Configuration Relevance in the Sales Order Segment (APO)

For variant configuration and the VC-configuration relevance the requirements strategy 'make-to-order' is required.

If the CDP-configuration scheme is used on APO side more details for the configuration exist – the valuations and the requirements.

Fig. 5.9. Sales Order with CDP-Configuration Relevance (APO)

The configuration of the sales order is transferred as valuation for CDP as shown in figure 5.9. The requirements (for the characteristic, see chapter 11) of the sales order are blank.

5.3 Object Dependencies

5.3.1 Structure and Usage of Object Dependencies

Object dependencies are used in R/3 to influence the explosion of the BOM and the routing depending on characteristic values. The most common types of object dependencies are selection conditions and procedures. Selection conditions control e.g. whether an item of a BOM is required depending on the value of a characteristic. Procedures on the other hand allow to influence the value of a characteristic depending on the value of another characteristic.

The object dependencies are either created as a separate entity with the transaction CU01 or within the BOM resp. routing itself. The creation of the object dependency as a separate entity has the advantage that it can be assigned to many different objects. The logic for the dependency is maintained in the dependency editor as coding as shown in figure 5.10.

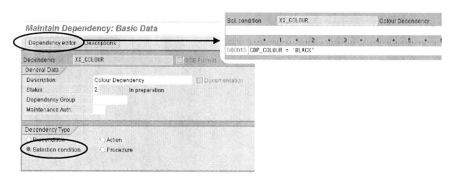

Fig. 5.10. Object Dependency (Selection Condition) (R/3)

Optionally a dependency group can be assigned to the dependency. For some cases the use of the dependency groups SAPAPOACT and SAPAPOOPR is mandatory to ensure the correct integration to APO. These cases are described in chapter 5.4.4 about reference characteristics and 8.3 about block planning. Object dependency groups are maintained in customising with the path

> *Logistics - General → Variant Configuration → Dependencies → Maintain Groups.*

In the example of figure 5.10 the selection condition is applied if the value of the characteristic is 'BLACK'. The object dependency is assigned to the BOM resp. the routing as shown in figure 5.11.

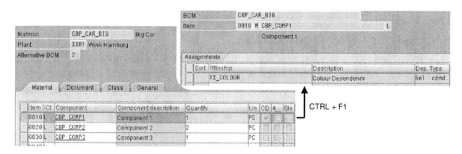

Fig. 5.11. Assignment of the Object Dependency to the BOM (R/3)

Alternatively the object dependency can be maintained within the BOM or the routing as shown in figure 5.12. In this case the logic applies only to that master data.

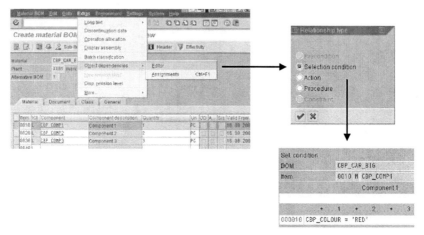

Fig. 5.12. Example for Object Dependencies (Selection) in the BOM (R/3)

In this example the component CBP_COMP1 is selected if the value for the colour of the header product CBP_CAR_BIG is 'RED'.

• *Object Variables*
Object variables define the BOM-level for which a selection condition or a statement of a procedure is applied. $SELF defines the current level, $PARENT one level above and $ROOT the top level – the level on which the configuration was entered. Only in the case of a multi-level configuration $ROOT and $PARENT will provide different results.

• *Syntax for Object Dependencies*
The syntax for the check and the assignment of characteristic values depends on the data type of the characteristic. Alphanumeric character values are assigned in quotation marks, numeric values without. Decimal places are maintained as a decimal point (e.g. 3.14). The operators '=', '<>', 'AND', 'OR', 'NOT' and 'IF' are supported among others.

• *Object Dependencies Check*
The object dependencies for a BOM or a routing (task list) can be checked in R/3 with transaction CU50 as shown in figure 5.13 without having to create a sales order.

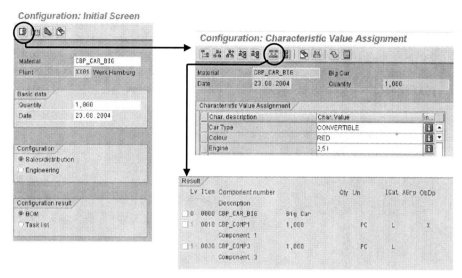

Fig. 5.13. Check for the Object Dependencies in R/3

For object dependencies of the type procedure it is possible to create separate functions as described later in this chapter.

• *Integration of the Object Dependencies with APO*
Object dependencies within the BOM or the routing are transferred to APO – both for the VC- and the CDP-configuration relevance. This integration requires the master data object PDS. The PPM does not support the integration of object dependencies. Figure 5.14 shows how the selection condition as maintained in the object dependencies (see figure 5.12) looks like in the PDS in APO.

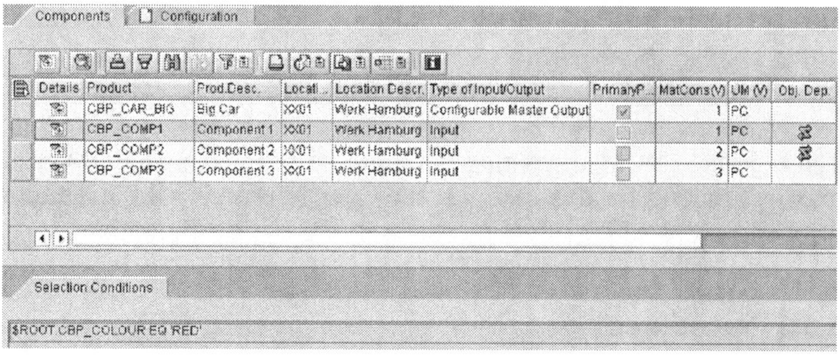

Fig. 5.14. Object Dependencies in the PDS in APO

The syntax of the object dependencies as displayed in the PDS is slightly different from R/3. Analogous to the object dependencies check in R/3 it is possible to simulate the impact of a configuration within APO. As shown in figure 5.15, for this purpose the 'configuration'-tab within the PDS display (transaction /SAPAPO/CURTO_SIMU) can be used.

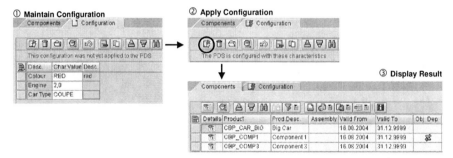

Fig. 5.15. Simulation of a Configuration in APO

For the display of the result one has to navigate to the respective objects (components, modes or activities) within the PDS.

5.3.2 Selection Conditions

A selection condition controls whether an item of a BOM or an operation of a routing is used for a given configuration, e.g. if the value of the characteristic CBP_COLOUR is 'BLACK':

```
CBP_COLOUR = 'BLACK'
```

resp. if it is 'BLACK' or 'GREY':

```
CBP_COLOUR = 'BLACK' OR CBP_COLOUR = 'GREY'
```

The objects – BOM or routing – should be the maximal BOM resp. the maximal routing for this case, i.e. they should contain all the components resp. operations which might be necessary for any configuration.

5.3.3 Procedures

Procedures are used to set the value of a characteristic e.g. depending on another characteristic value

```
$SELF.CBP_COLOUR = 'RED' IF $ROOT.CBP_SIZE = 'X'.
```

or to propagate the characteristic value from the finished product to the component:

```
$SELF.CBP_COLOUR = $ROOT.CBP_COLOUR.
```

The syntax for multiple assignments is

```
$SELF.CBP_COLOUR = 'RED'  IF $ROOT.CBP_SIZE = 'X',
$SELF.CBP_COLOUR = 'BLUE' IF $ROOT.CBP_SIZE = 'Y'.
```

5.3.4 Procedures with Reference Characteristics

Using reference characteristics it is possible to overrule master data settings by characteristic values, e.g. the quantity for a BOM item. Reference characteristics are 'normal' characteristics which have a link to the master data table and field on the 'additional data'-view as shown in figure 5.16.

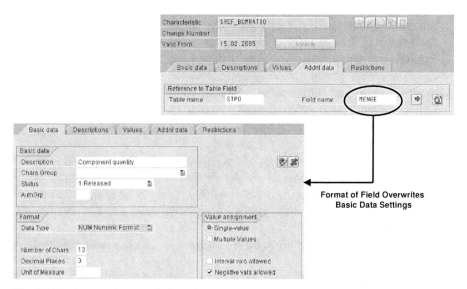

Fig. 5.16. Reference Characteristic (R/3)

The format and the description of the characteristic is taken from the referenced field. After saving the characteristic it is not possible to change the reference anymore. The reference characteristic has to be transferred to APO.

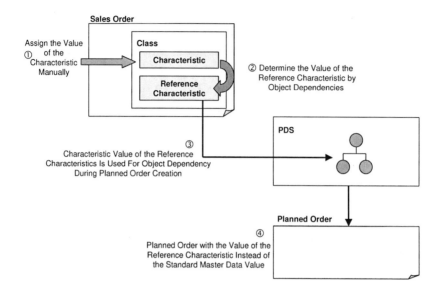

Fig. 5.17. Scheme for the Use of Reference Characteristics

Figure 5.17 shows the scheme for the use of reference characteristics. The reference characteristic is calculated by object dependencies, i.e. per default the flag 'not ready for input' is set in the characteristic to inhibit a manual maintenance during characteristic value assignment in the sales order. The value of the reference characteristic is used during the planned order creation and replaces the standard value of the PDS for that order. Object dependencies have to exist in order to take the value of the reference characteristic into account.

• *Dependency Group for Object Dependencies*
For dependencies for operations the dependency group SAPAPOOPR, for activities the dependency group SAPAPOACT has to be assigned to the dependency. The dependency group is maintained in the R/3 customising with the path

> *Logistics General → Variant Configuration → Dependencies → Maintain Groups.*

This is necessary to map the dependency from the operation in R/3 to the right entity in APO – mode, operation or activity.

• *Mapping of Reference Characteristics*

For the transfer of the reference characteristics to APO it is necessary to map the fields and tables as described in note 610873. The mapping table is found in the APO customising with the path

> *APO → Master Data → Classification and Configuration → Map Object Characteristics.*

Figure 5.18 shows an example for this mapping.

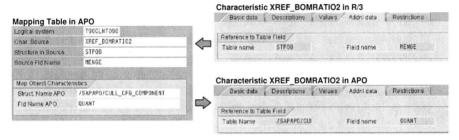

Fig. 5.18. Mapping of Reference Characteristics

Table 5.1 lists correspondencies for some common fields as the BOM item quantity (STPOB-MENGE), the standard value for an operation[1] (PLPO-VGW02) and the set-up group (PLPO-RFGRP). The set-up group can not be mapped without the use of variant functions (see also chapter 11.2.3).

Table 5.1. Correspondence Between R/3 and APO-Fields

R/3		APO	
Table	Field	Structure	Field
STPOB	MENGE	/SAPAPO/CULL_CFG_COMPONENT	QUANT
PLPO	VGW02[1]	/SAPAPO/CULL_CFG_MODE_PRODUCE	DURVAR
PLPO	RFGRP	/SAPAPO/CULL_CFG_ACT_ALL	GROUP_ID[2]
PLPO	RFSCH	/SAPAPO/CULL_CFG_ACT_ALL	ITEM_ID[2]

[1] using the standard value key SAP1 for machine time
[2] internal key; additional mapping with variant functions required

The settings for the mapping have to be done before the transfer of the reference characteristics since it is not possible to change the reference to the tables within the characteristic anymore. For the overruling of PDS components using reference characteristic note 815018 has to be considered.

5.3.5 Variant Functions

Variant functions allow to model complex dependencies using function modules with ABAP coding. This way it is possible to use information that is not included in the characteristics. An example for the use of a variant function is given in chapter 11 for the characteristic based determination of the set-up group.

The variant function references a function module (via the identical name) and is called by the object dependency. The variant function and the function module have to be created manually both in R/3 and in APO. Though the variant function and the function module are only evaluated in APO, the object dependencies are maintained in R/3 and for consistency reasons the variant function and the function module have to exist in R/3 as well. It is however sufficient to create a function module without source code in R/3 (especially if function modules and tables are used which are only available in APO) as long as no re-explosion of the master data is performed in R/3. Figure 5.19 visualises the structure of these entities:

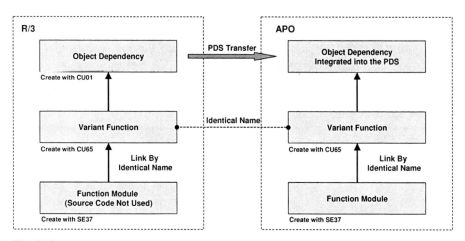

Fig. 5.19. Structure Overview for Variant Functions

Note that the variant functions in R/3 and APO must have the same name.

• *Function Module*
Function modules are created with transaction SE37 and are assigned to a function group. The function group is created on the same screen via the menu path *Goto → Function Groups → Create Group*. The function module for the variant functions requires the import parameter
        GLOBALS LIKE CUOV_00
the tables

```
QUERY LIKE CUOV_01
MATCH LIKE CUOV_01
```
and the exceptions
```
FAIL
INTERNAL_ERROR
```
where the table QUERY contains the data for the import characteristics that is provided by the function resp. the object dependency to the function module and the table MATCH contains the data that will be passed back to the function and the object dependency. The structure CUOV_01 contains the fields VARNAM for the name of the characteristic, ATFOR for the format of the value, ATWRT for the value as a characteristic and ATFLV for the numeric value. The online documentation provides additional information.

• *Variant Function*
The variant functions define the characteristics which are used as an input and those that will change their values. Variant functions are created with the transaction CU65, and figure 5.20 shows their maintenance.

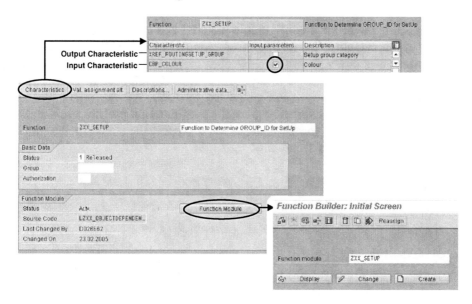

Fig. 5.20. Variant Functions (R/3 and APO)

Note that the input characteristics require the flag 'input parameter'. The maintenance of the variant function requires a status. For its use in the object dependencies the status has to be '1' (released). In APO the statuses 'released', 'in preparation' and 'locked' might not exist as entries in the table CUVFUN_ST. Note 601255 explains how to maintain the required entries.

• *Use of Variant Function in the Object Dependency*
To call a variant function VARFUNC in a procedure with the input characteristic INCHAR and the output characteristic OUTCHAR the following syntax is required:

```
FUNCTION VARFUNC
   (INCHAR  = $ROOT.INCHAR,
    OUTCHAR = $SELF.OUTCHAR)
```

For the input characteristics the values have to be derived from the entry point of the valuation.

5.4 Multi-Level Configuration

If the component for a configurable material is a configurable material as well (item category 'N' in the BOM required), the configuration for the component is either determined by object dependencies, by fix value assignment from the material master or interactively assigned in the sales order. All the three options are supported by APO. For the interactive assignment of the characteristic values the configuration profiles for both the finished product and the component must support the single or the multi-level BOM explosion, figure 5.21.

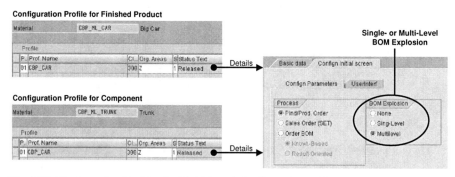

Fig. 5.21. Configuration Profiles for Multi-Level Configuration (R/3)

Unless a set is configured, the 'planned order' process should be selected. The characteristic value assignment in the sales order is performed per material as shown in figure 5.22.

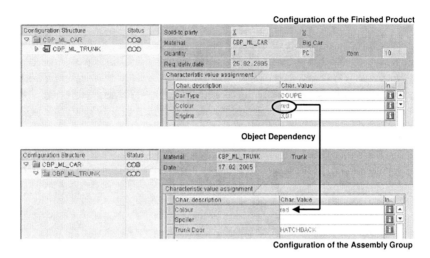

Fig. 5.22. Multi-Level Characteristic Value Assignment in the Sales Order (R/3)

Object dependencies and fix values are taken into account. The valuations for both the sales order and the dependent demand are transferred to APO, figure 5.23.

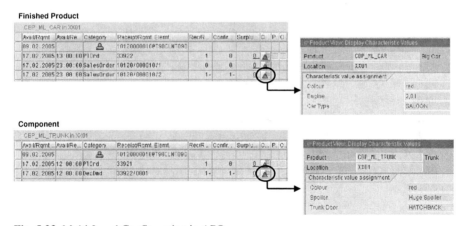

Fig. 5.23. Multi-Level Configuration in APO

The dependent demand is in the customer order segment of the sales order.

5.5 Configuration via Material Class

An alternative approach to select components depending on the character-istic value of the finished product is the use of material classes for config-urable materials (class type 200) instead of object dependencies. The basic idea is that the components have characteristic values assigned (of the class type 200 since the components are not configurable) and are selected according to the characteristic values of the sales order for the finished product. Figure 5.24 provides an overview about the required settings.

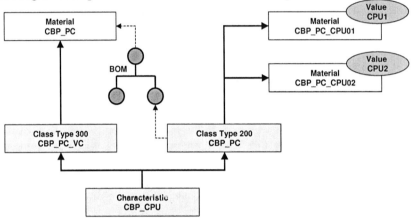

Fig. 5.24. Characteristic Assignments for Variant Configuration via Material Class

The configuration of the sales order causes the selection of the component with the same characteristic value – i.e. if the sales order is configured with the value 'CPU1', then the component CBP_PC_CPU01 is selected. This is possible because the material class (type 200) is assigned to the BOM instead of the individual components.

For the assignment of the material class to the BOM, the class must have the indicator to allow its use in the BOM, figure 5.25.

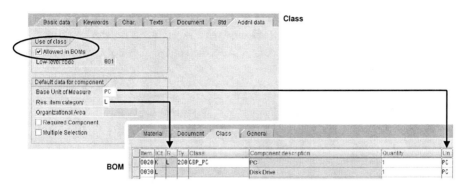

Fig. 5.25. Class Assignment to the BOM (R/3)

The material classes for configurable materials do not have to be transferred to APO. During the transfer of the PDS the fix characteristic value of the component (that is set in the material master of the component) is interpreted as an object dependency and transformed into selection criteria as shown in figure 5.26.

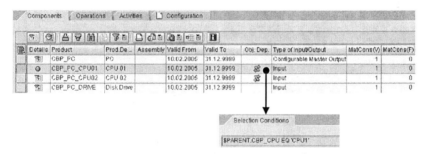

Fig. 5.26. PDS for Variant Configuration via Material Class (APO)

No object dependencies are required in R/3 for this approach.

5.6 Material Variants

The idea for the use of material variants is to produce common configurations of a configurable product as make-to-stock. This has the advantage of faster response to customer demands and offers the possibility to level fluctuations in the resource utilisation.

● *Master Data for Material Variants*
The material variants have a reference to a configurable product (for which a configuration profile must exist). The material variants are no configur-

able products (i.e. they are not of the type KMAT) nor do they have any class assignments. In the MRP3-view of the material master the link to the configurable product is maintained and the material is configured as shown in figure 5.27.

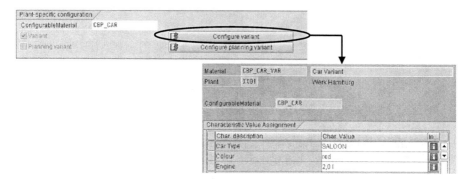

Fig. 5.27. Definition of a Material Variant (R/3)

To create a production version for the material variant it is necessary to create a reference to the BOM and to the routing of the configured material. For the BOM this is performed with the transaction CS40 as shown in figure 5.28.

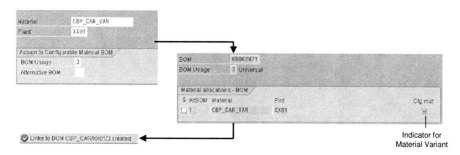

Fig. 5.28. Assignment of the Material Variant to the BOM of the Configured Material (R/3)

Only the material variant is entered in this transaction. The link to the BOM is found via the referenced configurable material. In the routing of the configurable material (transaction CA02) the material variant is assigned via the 'material assignment'-button as shown in figure 5.29.

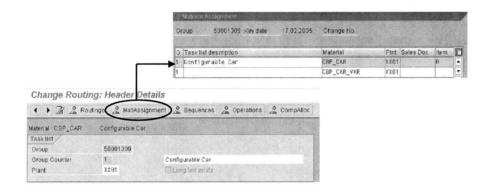

Fig. 5.29. Assignment of the Material Variant to the Routing of the Configured Material

With these prerequisites the production version for the material variant is created and transferred as a PDS. The components which have a selection condition for different characteristic values are filtered during the transfer.

● *Material Substitution in the Sales Order*
During the sales order process the entered configuration is checked against existing material variants and – depending on the settings in the item category – either a notification appears or the product is automatically substituted, figure 5.30.

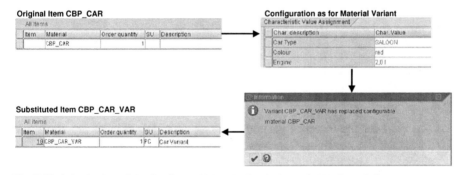

Fig. 5.30. Substitution of the Configured Material by the Material Variant (R/3)

With the substitution of the configurable product by the material variant the complete process is switched from make-to-order to make-to-stock.

● *Material Variants in APO*

The material variants in APO still have the link to the configured product as shown in figure 5.31.

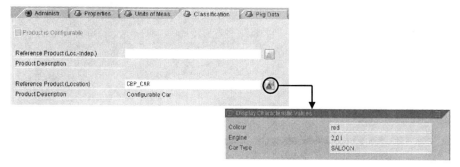

Fig. 5.31. Product Master for Material Variants in APO

In the product view the triangle is displayed that indicates characteristics, but without colour. Though the configuration is stored, the characteristics are not used for planning for the material variants.

Fig. 5.32. Product View for Material Variants in APO

The PDS for the material variant is the same as the PDS of the configured product if the configuration was applied. The object dependencies are displayed if they are applied for the configuration.

5.7 Configurable Material Variants

For the configurable material variants the variant is not completely configured (i.e. not all characteristic values are maintained) in the material master – the missing configuration is performed in the sales order. The business case for the use of configurable material variants is very different from the use of 'normal' material variants. The motivation to use configurable material variants is to reduce the effort of maintaining the characteristic values for the configuration and to reduce the effort of master data maintenance – especially for changes.

The sales order is placed for the configurable material variant, and therefore the order is already pre-configured. Usually only a certain percentage of the order is pre-configured, and the missing characteristic values are maintained as for the normal variant configuration, see figure 5.33.

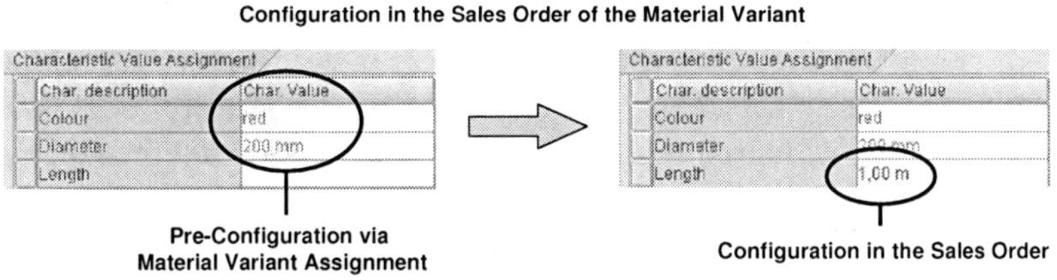

Configuration in the Sales Order of the Material Variant

Pre-Configuration via
Material Variant Assignment

Configuration in the Sales Order

Fig. 5.33. Sales Order for the Configurable Material Variant

Using configurable material variants no material substitution takes place nor would it be desirable. A typical case for the use of configurable material variants are the mill industries, where a quantity related property is maintained as a characteristic – e.g. the length of a tube. This case implies that the length has to be maintained as a configuration in the sales order.

• *Settings for the Use of Configurable Material Variants*
Though the material variant is configured in the sales order, the configurable material variant is not of the type configurable material (KMAT) and the indicator for 'material is configurable' is not set. The difference is that the item category has to support configuration (standard item category TAC resp. item category group 0002) and that the requirements class has to contain the setting that the configuration is mandatory (standard requirements class 046). If the configuration is not mandatory, the configuration screen does not appear since no configuration profile exists.

If the CDP-configuration scheme is used (which is the usual case since configurable material variants are mostly used in the mill industries), for the integration of the PDS for the configurable material variant the BAdI /SAPAPO/CURTO_CREATE has to be implemented. In the method VARIANT_WITH_OWN_VALUATION the statement

```
EV_DIFFERENT_COMPONENT_VALUES = 'X'.
```

needs to be added.

• *Configurable Material Variants in APO*

The configurable material variants look in APO the same as configurable products. In the product master the link to the configurable material exists like for the 'normal' material variants.

5.8 Variant Tables

Variant tables are used to maintain non-linear dependencies between different characteristics. Differing from normal tables, the variant tables can be used for the object dependencies (without the necessity to use variant functions). The variant tables are created in two steps: First the table is defined with the key characteristics as shown in figure 5.34.

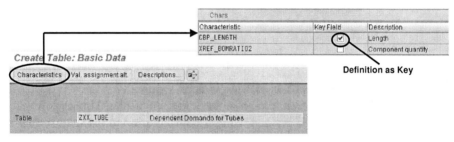

Fig. 5.34. Definition of the Variant Table (R/3 and APO)

The table and its characteristics are defined with the transaction CU61. The maintenance of the values for the table is performed with the transaction CU60, figure 5.35.

Table Maintenance

Table	ZXX_TUBE	Dependent Demands for Tubes
Length	Component quantity	
1,00 m	1,000	
2,00 m	3,000	
2,50 m	5,000	

Fig. 5.35. Table Maintenance for Variant Tables (R/3 and APO)

The syntax to assign a value from the variant table VARTAB to the characteristic CHAR depending on the value of the key characteristic KEYCHAR in the object dependencies is

```
TABLE VARTAB
   (   CHAR = CHAR,
     KEYCHAR = $SELF.KEYCHAR)
```

The variant table has to be created in R/3 and in APO as well before transferring the PDS. If the statuses for the variant table definition are missing, they have to be created explicitely as described in note 614280.

6 Make-to-Order with VC and Demand Planning

6.1 Make-to-Order with VC and Planning Overview

The motivation to combine the variant configuration with the demand planning is to plan the demands for the assembly groups based on the demand for the finished product. This implies that demand planning has to include the characteristic values as planning levels – which is enabled by the use of characteristic based forecasting (CBF).

Since the configurable materials have usually a make-to-order strategy, the forecast on finished product level is not used for the production of the finished product but for the production of the assembly groups (resp. the procurement of components). APO offers two alternative ways to apply CBF: One is to perform the production planning for the finished product in an inactive planning version and to transfer the dependent demand as forecast for the assembly group to the active version. The other alternative is to release the forecast with the characteristic value assignment to the planning segment of the active version. Figure 6.1 shows the overview about these two scenarios again.

Scenario	Demand Planning	Sales	Production
MTO with Variant Configuration and Planning in Inactive Version	Characteristic Based Forecasting	Multi-Level ATP or Capable-to-Promise	Production Planning with Characteristics
MTO with Variant Configuration and Planning in Active Version	Characteristic Based Forecasting	Forecast Check and/or Allocation Check	Production Planning with Characteristics

Fig. 6.1. Scenarios for Make-to-Order with Variant Configuration and Planning

The first alternative is available since APO 3.0 and therefore the more often used. The second alternative is available since APO 4.0 and requires the CDP-configuration scheme with its restrictions regarding planned order transfer and performance when using many characteristics (see chapter 11). The target industry for the first alternative is engineering, automotive and high tech/consumer goods, while the target for the second alternative is the mill industries.

6.2 Characteristic Based Forecasting

Characteristic based forecasting (CBF) is a functionality of Demand Planning. This leads us to a problem in the terminology because the term 'characteristic' is used in two ways:

1. characteristics as used within this book so far, i.e. an attribute to the product resp. the order and
2. characteristic as a basic object for Demand Planning which defines levels of planning (e.g. product, location, sales organisation etc.). The actual planning is performed for characteristic value combinations (CVCs), which are the master data for Demand Planning.

For the purpose of distinction the first type of characteristics is called 'configuration-characteristic' and the second 'info object-characteristic' whenever necessary. Consequently, in the case of CBF the demand planning is carried out on configuration-characteristic level, where the configuration-characteristic is used as info object-characteristic. Still not confused?

● *Planning Object Structure for CBF*
In the basic configuration for demand planning the main prerequisite is that the flag for CBF is set in the basic planning object structure. This controls that the three info object-characteristics 9AMV_PROF, 9AMV_TAB and 9AMV_ROW are included as shown in figure 6.2.

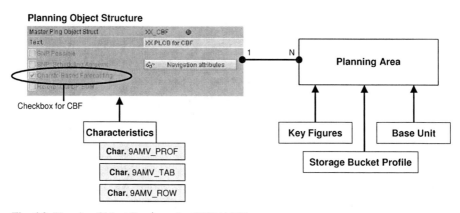

Fig. 6.2. Planning Object Structure for CBF (APO)

Those info object-characteristics provide the link to the CBF-profile and the CBF-table.

The only difference for the planning area is that if a key figure shall have the option for fixing, the second key figure for the fixed values must be added to the planning area manually.

• *CBF-Profile and CBF-Table Overview*
CBF-profile and CBF-table are master data which are linked to the product and define the combination of the configuration-characteristics which may be used for this product in Demand Planning as info-object characteristic value combinations (in addition to the already existing, non-configuration based CVCs). Figure 6.3 provides an overview about the dependencies of CBF-profile and CBF-table to the other objects.

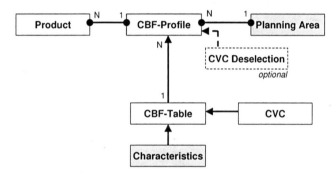

Fig. 6.3. CBF-Profile and CBF-Table (APO)

For each product a CBF-profile has to be created, but a product can only be assigned to one CBF-profile. One CBF-table can be assigned to more than one CBF-profile. Both the CBF-profile and the CBF-table are maintained in the integrated CBF-profile maintenance.

• *CBF-Table*
In the CBF-profile maintenance with transaction /SAPAPO/IPM01 you can choose between a product, a planning area or a CBF-table. After choosing 'CBF-table', first the name for the CBF-table has to be defined and then the configuration-characteristics have to be assigned to the table as shown in figure 6.4.

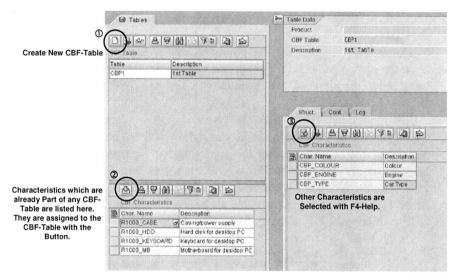

Fig. 6.4. CBF-Table – Assignment of Characteristics (APO)

The definition of the relevant characteristic value combinations (CVCs) in the CBF-profile is done either interactively for explicit CVCs or is generated from a subset of characteristic values as shown in figure 6.5:

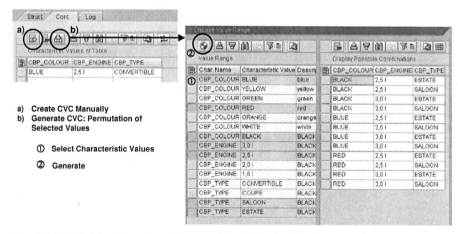

Fig. 6.5. CBF-Table – Creation of Characteristic Value Combinations (APO)

The defined combination of values for configuration-characteristics will be used as planning levels in Demand Planning, i.e. for those CVCs planning will be possible. The total number of CVCs in Demand Planning (per product) will be the number of the CVCs from the CBF-profile times the number of CVCs without consideration of configuration-characteristics.

● *CBF-Profile*

The CBF-profile is created with the same transaction /SAPAPO/IPM01. In this case 'product' has to be chosen and the product has to be specified. For the maintenance of the CBF-profile the following 5 steps must be performed:

1. create the CBF-profile
2. assign a planning area
3. activate the CBF-profile
4. assign a CBF-table
5. optionally: deselect CVCs from the CBF-table.

Figure 6.6 shows the CBF-profile maintenance.

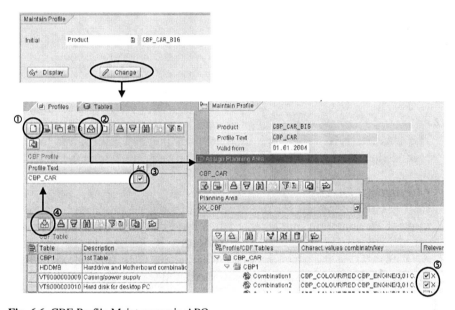

Fig. 6.6. CBF-Profile Maintenance in APO

The CBF-profile needs to be created before the characteristic value combinations are maintained.

● *Characteristic Value Combinations in DP*

By creating the CBF-profile and assigning it to the product the values for the info object-characteristics 9AMV_PROF (CBF-profile), 9AMV_TAB (CBF-table) and 9AMV_ROW (characteristic base) are populated. Figure 6.7 shows the characteristic value combinations (CVC) for the planning object structure as displayed with transaction /SAPAPO/MC62.

APO - Loca	APO Product	CBF Profil	Char.-Base	CBF Table
XX01	CBP_CAR_BIG	35	1	3457
XX01	CBP_CAR_BIG	35	2	3457
XX01	CBP_CAR_BIG	35	3	3457

Fig. 6.7. Characteristic Value Combination for Planning Object Structure

The characteristic values for the CBF-profile, CBF-table and characteristic base provide the link to the characteristic profile. This way the configuration-characteristic values are planned for even though the info object-characteristic value combinations are different. If no CBF-profile exists, the CVCs are not created for a CBF-relevant planning object structure.

• *Master Data Changes*
For the change of the info-object characteristics, for example if a new product is added. In this case the difference to the normal process of characteristic value maintenance is that additionally the CBF-profile has to be created for the product.

• *Demand Planning with Configuration-Characteristics*
The characteristic values are used in planning and navigation just like normal characteristics – including drill down and selection in the shuffler.

• *Limitations for CBF*
CBF is only supported for the planning of finished products because the forecast consumption on characteristics level does not work with dependent demands. The number of key figures is limited to 20 including APODPDANT in the planning book when using CBF (the number of key figures for the planning area is not limited) and the disaggregation type 'N' (no disaggregation) is not supported. See note 484144 for more information. The results of CBF can only be used in PP/DS and not in SNP.

6.3 Forecast Release and Forecast Consumption

In the following we describe the alternatives for the forecast release and the forecast consumption in general – i.e. not only the functions that are used in the two scenarios for make-to-order with variant configuration and planning, but also for the scenario 'sales order oriented planning'.

• *Forecast Release*

The release of the forecast needs to be done in different ways depending on the scenario. One of the main distinguishing features is whether for each CVC a separate forecast is released or whether the CVCs are aggregated and the forecast is released only with the class information. If separate forecasts per CVC are released, the forecast consumption is performed on CVC-level as well. To control the creation of separate forecasts per CVC a consumption group has to be defined and assigned to the product master and maintained in the release settings. For the scenario using the VC-configuration scheme the forecast is released in an aggregated way, for the scenario using the CDP-configuration scheme and the scenario 'sales order oriented planning' using descriptive characteristics the consumption group is applied to create separate forecasts per CVC. Another differentiator is whether the forecast is released to the planning segment or to the make-to-stock segment, which is controlled by the requirements strategy in the product master or as a setting in the release job. If a make-to-stock scenario is used, the release has to be done to the make-to-stock segment, which requires a BAdI for the scenarios with CDP-configuration relevance (there is no make-to-stock scenario for the VC-configuration relevance, though the forecast is released to the make-to-stock segment but to an inactive version). Note that an integration of planned and production orders with configuration with a make-to-stock strategy is only possible with IS Mill. Figure 6.8 provides an overview about the different options.

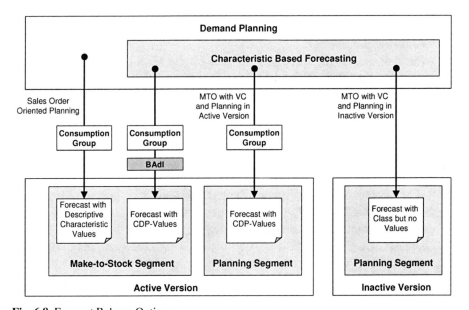

Fig. 6.8. Forecast Release Options

If CBF is used, then for the release with consumption group to the active version the CDP-configuration relevance is required. The release to the inactive version is done with the VC-configuration relevance.

Figure 6.9 shows the different representation of the characteristics in the forecast – depending whether only descriptive characteristics, the CDP-configuration relevance or the VC-configuration relevance is used.

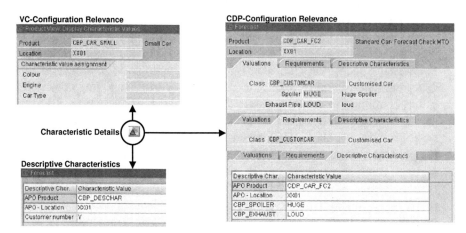

Fig. 6.9. Characteristic Details for Forecasts – Different Configuration Relevance (APO)

The green triangle as the indicator for characteristics is displayed for all the three kinds of the forecast.

• Consumption Group
After the release, the forecast is usually on the level of the product and the location only. This is the level the forecast consumption takes place as well. With the consumption group it is possible to have separate lines per characteristic value combination for a forecast. For the forecast consumption the characteristics which are used in demand planning are assigned to fields from the sales order. The consumption group is maintained with the transaction /SAPAPO/CSP1 per planning area and assigned to the product master and the release settings.

For the scenario 'sales order oriented planning' the 'normal' info object-characteristics from DP are used as descriptive characteristics. In this example we want to consume the forecast on customer level. Therefore the characteristic CUSTOMER has been included into the basic planning object structure. This characteristic has to be assigned now to the field KUNNR of the sales order. Figure 6.10 shows the settings for the consumption group for this example.

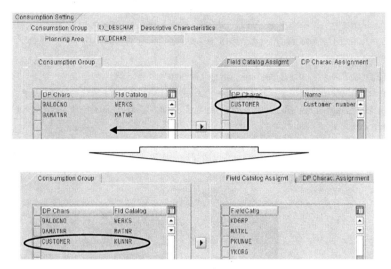

Fig. 6.10. Consumption Group for Descriptive Characteristics (APO)

For CBF the consumption group is used as well, but not the info object-characteristics are now chosen but the configuration-characteristics. In the 'DP characteristic assignment'-view the configuration-characteristics that have been maintained in the CBF-profile are available, figure 6.11. The field catalogue assignment is carried out automatically.

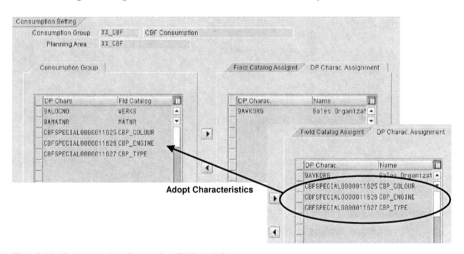

Fig. 6.11. Consumption Group for CBF (APO)

The forecast receives its configuration only via the vehicle of the descriptive characteristics. If forecast with CDP-characteristic relevance is used for planning or for the ATP check, the consumption group has always to be defined for the forecast release.

• *Assignment of the Consumption Group*
The consumption group has to be assigned to the 'demand'-view of the product master as shown in figure 6.12 and to the settings for the release of the forecast.

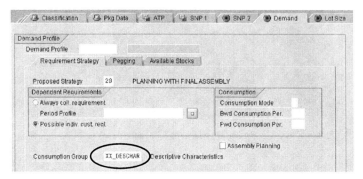

Fig. 6.12. Assignment of the Consumption Group to the Product Master (APO)

The assignment of the consumption group to the release settings (transaction /SAPAPO/MC90) is shown in figure 6.13.

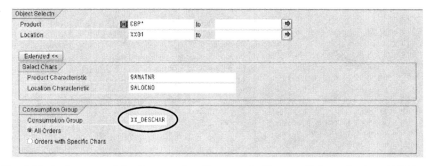

Fig. 6.13. Assignment of the Consumption Group to the Forecast Release Settings (APO)

The forecast is defined by locationproduct, planning segment and the descriptive characteristics. Therefore the consumption group is often required as well when accessing the forecast (e.g. for deletion reports), but not for the reorganisation with transaction /SAPAPO/MD74.

• *Release with Consumption Group to the Make-to-Stock Segment*
Though this is not part of any of the selected scenarios, it might be required to release the forecast with CDP-configuration relevance to the

make-to-stock segment (and have separate forecasts per CVC for planning and forecast consumption). This bears some limitations – e.g. it is not possible to transfer the planned orders to R/3 unless they are converted to production orders (each planned order with CDP-configuration relevance is converted into a production order in R/3). The setting to prevent the transfer of planned orders is on client level. Therefore this option should only be considered if planned orders are not required in R/3.

From a configuration point of view it is required to activate the BAdI /SAPAPO/DM_BADI_CONF and add following line of coding to the method CONFR_FILL:

```
method /SAPAPO/IF_EX_DM_BADI_CONF~CONFR_FILL.
  move 9 to et_stra_details-PLNVP .
endmethod.
```

None of the selected scenarios requires this option.

6.4 Scenario Description for Planning in Inactive Version

6.4.1 Process Chain for Planning in Inactive Version

The basic idea of this scenario is to use the demand planning information for the configured finished products to calculate the dependent demand for the non-configured components. This scenario is limited to a single-level configuration. The calculation of the dependent demand takes place in an inactive version, and the dependent demand from the inactive version is transferred as forecast for the components into the active version. Figure 6.14 shows the process chain for this scenario.

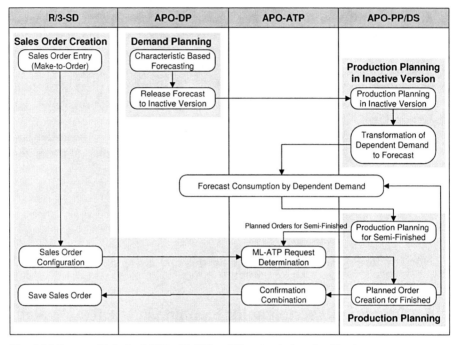

Fig. 6.14. Process Chain for MTO with VC and Planning in Inactive Version

Since this scenario was developed for the VC-configuration scheme we will describe the steps for the VC-configuration scheme only. Though it is technically possible to apply the CDP-configuration scheme (with minor deviations, especially for the release of the forecast) for this scenario as well, this would be rather unusual.

Demand planning is performed using CBF on finished product level including the characteristic values of the finished product. The forecast is released to an inactive planning version without any consumption group. For the first BOM-level production planning is performed in the inactive version, and the dependent demands are transformed as forecasts (i.e. planned independent requirements) for the assembly groups into the active version. These forecasts are the basis for the production or procurement of the assembly groups resp. components. If a sales order is placed, the forecast is consumed by the dependent demand.

The inactive planning version is used because with the VC-configuration scheme no forecast consumption is possible on characteristic level for the finished product. A release of the forecast to the active planning version is possible as well but would lead to an imprecise forecast consumption.

• *Demand Planning with Characteristics*

The finished products are planned for on characteristic value level in Demand Planning using the CBF functionality. As shown in figure 6.15, the only difference is that the planning takes place on configuration-characteristic level as well.

Info Object-Characteristic   Configuration-Characteristic

	Colour	Car Type	Unit	W 04.2005	W 05.2005	W 06.2005	W 07.2005	W 08.2005	W 09.2005	W
Forecast	Total	Total	PC	10	14	8	10	10	8	
	BLACK	Total	PC	4	4	2	4	4	2	
		ESTATE	PC	2	2	2	2		2	
		SALOON	PC	2	2		2	4		
	BLUE	Total	PC	4	4	2	4	2	3	
		ESTATE	PC	2	2	2	2	2	1	
		SALOON	PC	2	2		2		2	
	RED	Total	PC	2	6	4	2	4	1	
		SALOON	PC	2	6	4	2	4	1	

Fig. 6.15. Demand Planning with CBF (APO)

From a user's point of view the configuration-characteristics behave the same as the info-object characteristics.

• *Forecast Release*

In the next step the forecast is released into an inactive version. There are two points of attention:

- there must not be a consumption group neither in the settings for the release (transaction /SAPAPO/MC90) nor in the product master and
- the strategy for planning without final assembly (e.g. standard strategy 30) has to be maintained either in the settings for the release or in the product master.

As shown in the log of the release, only one forecast was released per locationproduct.

Display logs

Ty...	Message Text
○	Release: Forecast
○	Characteristic combination: CBP_CAR_SMALL XX01

Fig. 6.16. Log for the Release of the Forecast (APO)

The forecast contains the information about the class but not about the characteristic values. If more than one forecast exists within the same bucket but with different characteristic values, still only one forecast is released as shown in figure 6.17.

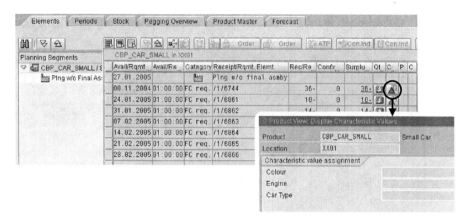

Fig. 6.17. Forecast after Release (APO)

Note that the values for the characteristics are blank and that there is only one forecast per bucket.

• *Production Planning in the Inactive Version*

For the production planning in the inactive version the standard heuristics are used. Since the planning procedure for multi-level ATP contains the heuristic SAP_PP_CTP which is not suited to cover demands, the production planning heuristic SAP_PP_002 must be included into the MRP heuristic explicitely.

As a prerequisite the PDS master data with the object dependencies is transferred from R/3. The result of the production planning run are planned orders which have the class assigned but no characteristic values as shown in figure 6.18 – analogous to the forecast.

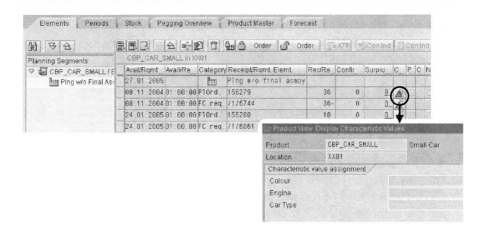

Fig. 6.18. Planned Order with VC-Configuration Relevance (Without Configuration)

The dependent demand for the components reflects however the characteristic values of the forecast. In this example the characteristic values of the forecast were 12 each for the colours 'BLACK', 'BLUE' and 'RED'. Component 1 is required for all colours, component 2 only for 'RED' and component 3 only for 'BLUE'. Figure 6.19 shows the dependent demand of the planned order.

Order	Product Requirements				
▽ In-house production 154768	Product	Prod.Descript.	F..	C..	Pr..	Reqm...
▽ Receipts	CBP_COMP1	Component 1			🖉	36-
CBP_CAR_SMALL	CBP_COMP2	Component 2			🖉	12-
▽ Requirements	CBP_COMP3	Component 3			🖉	12-
CBP_COMP1						
CBP_COMP2						
CBP_COMP3						

Fig. 6.19. Dependent Demand Reflecting the Characteristic Values of the Forecast

The characteristic values of the demand are taken into account because during the planned order creation the characteristic values are read from demand planning. The usage of a requirements strategy for planning without final assembly is required for this – else the characteristic values are not read from demand planning. The planned orders are not transferred to R/3 because they are in an inactive version.

● *Transformation of the Dependent Demand to a Forecast*
The purpose of the previous steps was to calculate the expected dependent demand for the assembly groups based on the forecast for the finished

products. The dependent demand for the assembly groups in the inactive version is transformed to a forecast for the assembly groups in the active version as described in the next chapter.

• *Sales Order Creation*
The sales order is created and configured as described in chapter 5 for make-to-order with variant configuration.

• *ATP Check and Production Planning*
Sensible alternatives for the ATP check are either the multi-level ATP or CTP. The purpose of the whole scenario is to create a better demand plan for the components which implies that the components might be bottlenecks. The basic properties of these and the resulting planned order creation is described in Dickersbach (2004).

• *Forecast Consumption by Dependent Demand*
The ATP check creates planned orders either via CTP or multi-level ATP. The dependent demand of the planned orders consume the forecast for the assembly groups.

6.4.2 System Configuration Determinants

For the make-to-order scenario with variant configuration and planning in an inactive version the VC-configuration scheme is required. On R/3-side a make-to-order strategy and a variant configuration class is required, figure 6.20.

Requirements Class Account Assignment	Class Type (R/3)	Configuration Scheme	Master Data
Make-to-Stock	Batch (023)	CDP	PPM
Make-to-Order	Variant Config. (300)	VC	PDS

Required / Supported
Supported but Unusual
Not Supported

Fig. 6.20. Determinants for MTO with VC and Planning in an Inactive Version

Since object dependencies are used, again the PDS master data object is mandatory. The PDS with object dependencies is transferred for the finished products. Though these will be used in an inactive version, it is not necessary to assign them explicitly to the inactive version.

6.4.3 Transformation of the Dependent Demand

Since the purpose of the previous steps is to calculate the demand for the assembly groups in order to trigger production, the dependent demand has to be transformed into a forecast for the assembly groups. The more tedious way to do so would be to transfer the dependent demand to a key figure in Demand Planning and release the key figure content to SNP into the active version. The shortcut for this process is to use the transaction /SAPAPO/DMP2 as shown in figure 6.21.

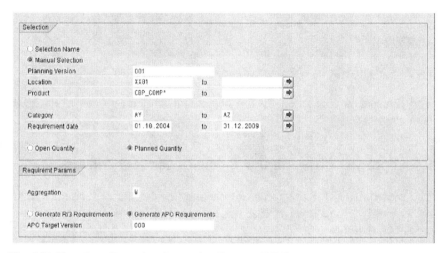

Fig. 6.21. Transform Dependent Demand to Forecast (APO)

The product selection has to contain the components. Only those components are selected which have a strategy for planning with final assembly (e.g. standard strategy 20) and are flagged for assembly planning. After a successful transformation the log displays the generated forecasts as shown in figure 6.22.

Date\User\Time	Numb
▽ ◉ 27.01.2005	4
▽ ◉ D026662	4
◉ 12:13.33	4

Ty.	Message Text	Det	Current Date	Time
◯	Generation of planned independent requirements - selection p...	◉	27.01.2005	12:13.33
◯	The time zone used is: UTC		27.01.2005	12:13.33
◯	Forecast generated successfully in APO		27.01.2005	12:13:33
◯	Generated planned independent requirements	◉	27.01.2005	12:13:37

Product	Location	Strategy	Time	Plan. qty	BUn	C	VS	RqTy	Active
CBP_COMP1	XX01	2Z	01.11.2004 12:00:00	36,000	W				
CBP_COMP1	XX01	2Z	17.01.2005 12:00:00	10,000	W				
CBP_COMP1	XX01	2Z	24.01.2005 12:00:00	14,000	W				

Fig. 6.22. Log for the Generation of Forecasts (APO)

The result of this step is the forecast for the components in the active version as shown in figure 6.23.

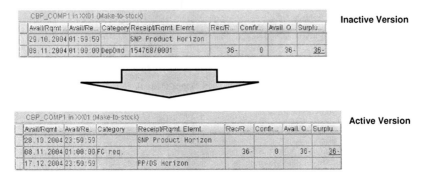

Fig. 6.23. Transformation of the Dependant Demand to Forecast (APO)

The forecast is consumed by the dependent demand as described in the next chapter.

6.4.4 Forecast Consumption by the Dependent Demand

The prerequisites for the forecast consumption by the dependent demand on assembly group level is that the components are planned as make-to-stock and that the

-   the requirements strategy allows planning with final assembly,
-   the checkbox for assembly planning is selected in the product master and
-   the dependent demands are collective requirements

as shown in figure 6.24.

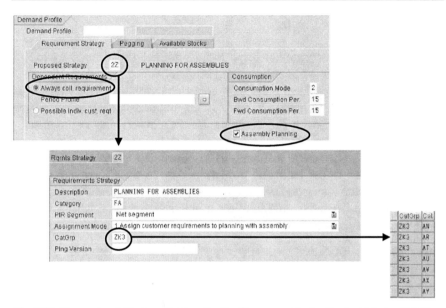

Fig. 6.24. Demand and Strategy Settings for the Component in the Product Master (APO)

Note that the ATP categories AY for the dependent demand and AU, AV and AX for the order reservation have to be included into the category group of the strategy.

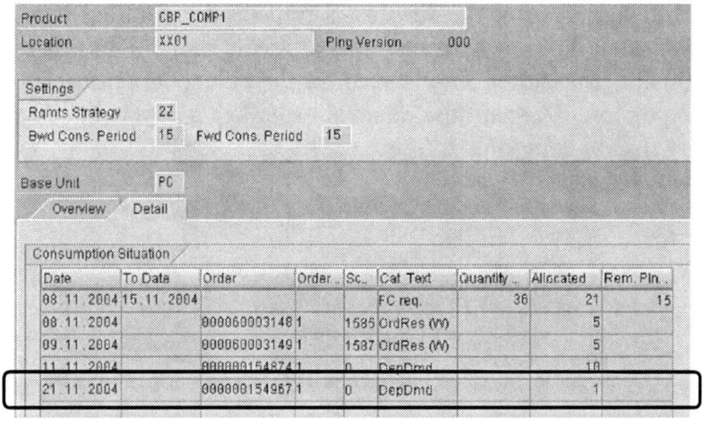

Fig. 6.25. Forecast Consumption for the Component (APO)

The consumption situation overview (transaction /SAPAPO/DMP1) shows that the forecast is consumed by the dependent demand of the planned order on the assembly group level as shown in figure 6.25.

6.4.5 Component Logic

The usage of the component logic is an optional functionality which is only possible for the VC-configuration scheme.

Demand Planning takes great care about consistency of the data across the different planning levels. In some cases this consistency is not desired – an example would be the planning for PCs where the components – CPUs, hard discs and others – are modelled as characteristics. These components can be used in different PCs. Since the customer demand is stronger related to the technical properties than to the PC-model, demand planning on characteristic level might be desired. Now one PC might have more than one hard disc, and to allow a planning for more hard discs than PCs an info object-characteristic value for the difference is introduced:

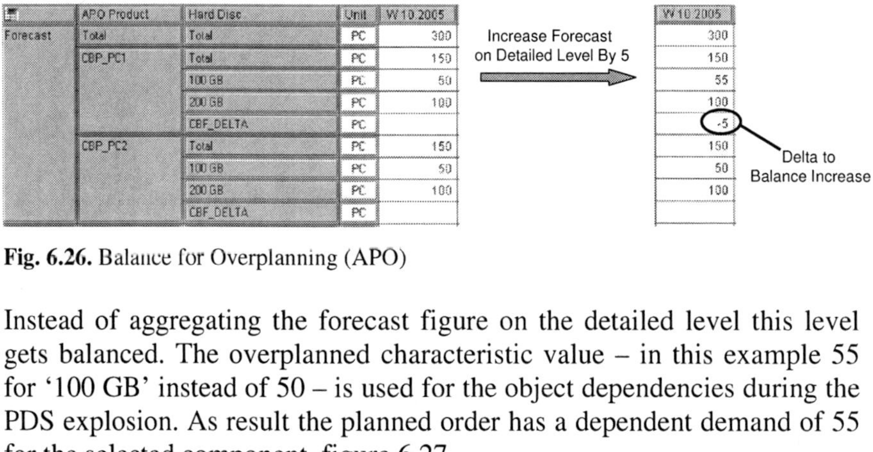

🔳	APO Product	Hard Disc	Unit	W 10 2005			W 10 2005
Forecast	Total	Total	PC	300	Increase Forecast		300
	CBP_PC1	Total	PC	150	on Detailed Level By 5		150
		100 GB	PC	50	⟹		55
		200 GB	PC	100			100
		CBF_DELTA	PC				-5
	CBP_PC2	Total	PC	150			150
		100 GB	PC	50			50
		200 GB	PC	100			100
		CBF_DELTA	PC				

Delta to Balance Increase

Fig. 6.26. Balance for Overplanning (APO)

Instead of aggregating the forecast figure on the detailed level this level gets balanced. The overplanned characteristic value – in this example 55 for '100 GB' instead of 50 – is used for the object dependencies during the PDS explosion. As result the planned order has a dependent demand of 55 for the selected component, figure 6.27.

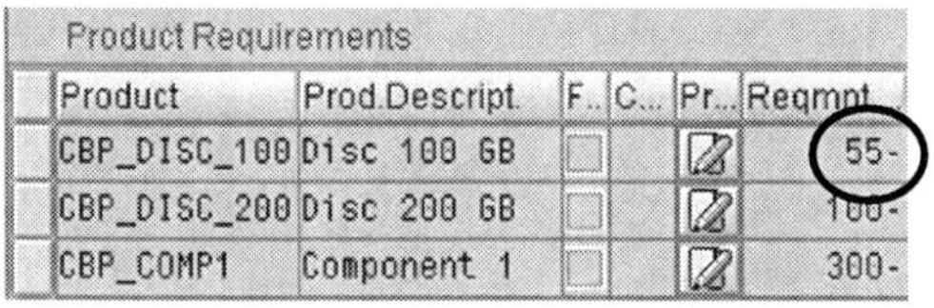

Product Requirements						
Product	Prod.Descript.	F..	C...	Pr...	Reqmnt
CBP_DISC_100	Disc 100 GB			🖉	55-
CBP_DISC_200	Disc 200 GB			🖉	100-
CBP_COMP1	Component 1			🖉	300-

Fig. 6.27. Dependent Requirements in the Planned Order Using Component Logic (APO)

• *Settings in the CBF-Profile for the Use of the Component Logic*
The prerequisite for this behaviour is that in the CBF-profile the settings for the component logic are made. The maintenance of these settings is more stable with the old transaction /SAPAPO/DPC1 as shown in figure 6.28 step by step.

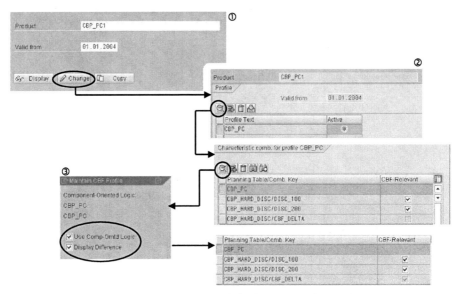

Fig. 6.28. Maintenance of the Component Logic in the CBF-Profile (APO)

When entering the CBF-profile, make sure that the 'valid from'-entry is maintained.

6.5 Scenario Description for Planning in Active Version

6.5.1 Process Chain for Planning in Active Version

This scenario was developed for and requires the use of the CDP-configuration scheme. The main difference to the previous scenario (planning in an inactive version) is that no inactive planning version is required. The planning of the finished product in order to determine the dependent demand for the assembly groups resp. the components is done in the planning segment of the active version. The reason for using the planning segment is that the production for the finished product is in most cases only started when a sales order is placed. Another reason is that planned orders (and production orders) with CDP-configuration relevance in the make-to-stock segment can not be integrated with R/3 unless IS Mill is used.

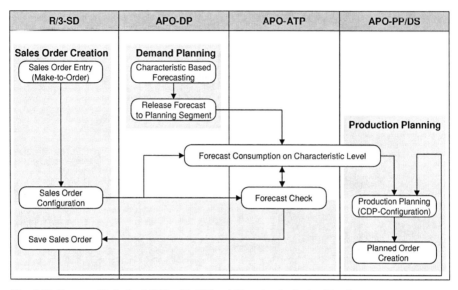

Fig. 6.29. Process Chain for MTO with VC and Planning in Active Version

The consequence of planning in the planning segment is that CTP can not be used any more as an ATP method (unless the resources are regarded as infinite). The planned orders in the planning segment would block the resource capacity for the CTP-planned orders in the sales order segment. On the other hand, due to the use of the CDP-configuration scheme separate forecast elements are created for each characteristic value combination. This allows the use of the forecast check on characteristic level. The process steps for the scenario 'make-to-order with variant configuration and planning in the active version' are shown in figure 6.29. Compared to the scenario 'make-to-order with variant configuration and planning in the inactive version', the forecast consumption is done on finished product level and no data copy between planning versions is required.

• *Demand Planning with Characteristics*
The finished products are planned on characteristic value in Demand Planning using the CBF functionality as in the previous scenario.

• *Forecast Release*
The forecast is now released to the active version and the consumption group needs to be maintained in the product master and in the release settings as described in chapter 6.3. An example for the log for the release of the forecast is shown in figure 6.30.

Fig. 6.30. Log for the Forecast Release with CDP-Configuration Relevance (APO)

Note that for each locationproduct and characteristic value combination an entry is listed in the log. Figure 6.31 shows the representation of the forecast in the product view.

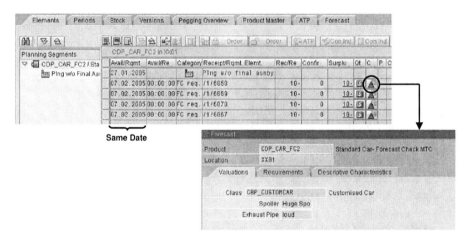

Fig. 6.31. Forecast with CDP-Configuration Relevance (APO)

With the CDP-configuration relevance the forecasts now have a valuation. The requirements are blank.

• Production Planning
Production planning is performed with the usual heuristics – no change in the set-up of the production planning is required for planning with the CDP-configuration relevance. Chapter 11 describes the properties in detail. Figure 6.32 shows the result of a production planning run in the product view.

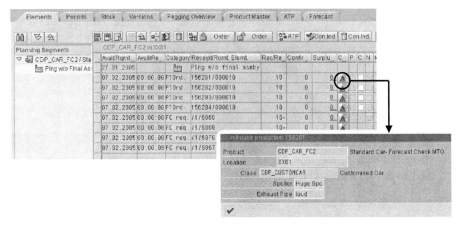

Fig. 6.32. Planned Orders with CDP-Configuration Relevance (APO)

In the pegging overview (transaction /SAPAPO/PEG1) it can be easily checked that only elements with the same valuations are pegged.

The production planning in the planning segment is required to create the receipt elements for the assembly groups resp. the components. The production planning in the planning segment might provide a feedback about the feasibility of the forecast – which is especially valuable for if the forecast check is used in the ATP. Another implication of the forecast check is that production planning is required for the sales orders.

• Sales Order Creation
For variant configuration make-to-order is usually applied, though make-to-stock would be possible in combination with the CDP-configuration scheme and the IS Mill solution as well. This case is described in chapter 8 about the scenario 'configure-to-order with propagation'. The configuration of the sales order is performed as in the processes before.

• ATP Check
The most suitable way to perform the ATP check in this scenario is the forecast check. The multi-level ATP check does not support the CDP-configuration scheme and CTP is not an option because it might lead to a double capacity consumption in combination with planning in the planning segment. The use of the forecast check implies that the forecasted quantities are feasible. The creation of the actual receipts needs to be done by the production planning run afterwards. As an alternative or in combination with the forecast check an allocation check is possible. Both options – the forecast check on characteristic level and the allocation check on characteristic level – are described in the next chapter.

6.5.2 System Configuration Determinants

For variant configuration with planning in the active version the CDP-configuration scheme and the PDS master data are mandatory. On R/3-side the make-to-order strategy is common, though make-to-stock is possible with some limitations as well (see chapter 8). The class type 300 is required on R/3-side.

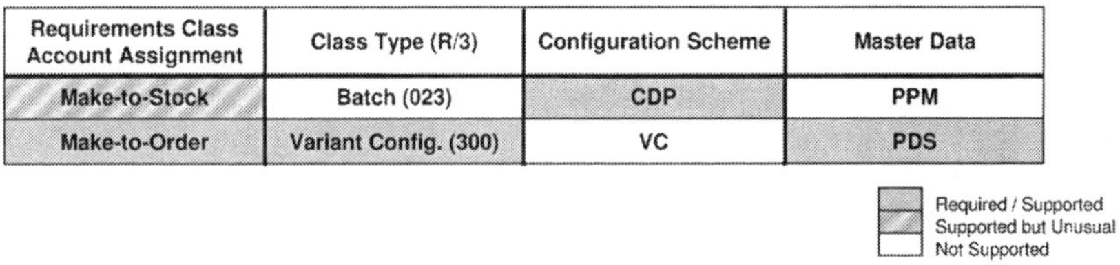

Requirements Class Account Assignment	Class Type (R/3)	Configuration Scheme	Master Data
Make-to-Stock	Batch (023)	CDP	PPM
Make-to-Order	Variant Config. (300)	VC	PDS

Required / Supported
Supported but Unusual
Not Supported

Fig. 6.33. Determinants for MTO with VC and Planning in the Active Version

The VC-configuration scheme can not be used because this scenario relies on separate forecasts per characteristics value combination. The use of the PDS is mandatory for the integration of object dependencies from R/3 – if this is not required, the PPM could be used as well.

6.5.3 Forecast Check on Characteristic Level

The forecast is released on detailed level using the consumption group and therefore the forecast check is performed on detailed level as well. To check the forecast for make-to-order in the planning segment the check mode needs to contain the assignment mode '2' (assign customer requirements to planning without assembly).

• Rules-Based ATP with Forecast Check
Generally it is possible to use rules-based ATP to perform a characteristic value substitution during the forecast check. There are however limitations regarding the use of rules-based ATP in combination with make-to-order as described in note 453921 – mainly due to the copying of the account assignment to the sub-items. Especially for the configuration with the CDP-configuration scheme there are additional problems in setting the configuration for the sub-items in R/3. Since the forecast check is used within the described scenarios only for make-to-order this option is not explained any further.

6.5.4 Allocation Check on Characteristic Level

The allocation check is usually performed on any field combination that is within the field object catalogue. Since the characteristics are freely defined, they are not part of the field object catalogue. To perform the allocation check nevertheless on characteristic level, the CBF-table is used instead of the field object catalogue.

In the product allocation group the checkbox 'use configuration characteristics' has to be selected to allow the assignment of the CBF-table to the allocation group, figure 6.34.

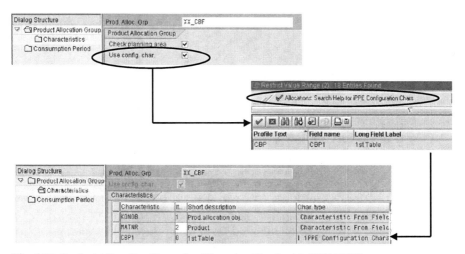

Fig. 6.34. Product Allocation Group for Allocation Check with CBF (APO)

To select the characteristic for the CBF-table via F4, the view with the values for the configuration objects (instead of the field catalogue) has to be selected.

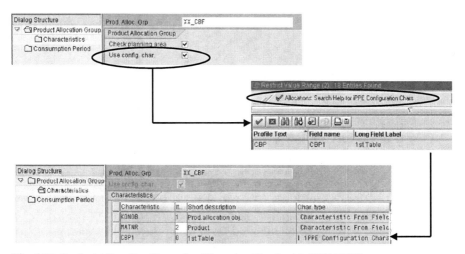

Fig. 6.35. Connection of the Allocation Group to the Planning Area (APO)

For the connection to the planning area an internal key for the CBF-table is generated. This has to be assigned to the characteristic 9AMV_TAB of the planning area (resp. the planning object structure) as shown in figure 6.35.

6.5.5 Forecast Consumption on Characteristic Level

For this scenario the consumption of a forecast in the planning segment by a sales order in the sales order segment is required. Therefore the check mode needs to have the assignment mode 'assign customer requirements to planning without final assembly' and the requirements strategy 30 has to be assigned. Figure 6.36 shows the forecast consumption on characteristic level.

Fig. 6.36. Forecast Consumption on Characteristic Level (APO)

7 Sales from Stock with Characteristics

7.1 Scenario Description

7.1.1 Process Chain

In some cases the result of the production might differ depending on uncontrollable factors. For example in chemical production processes (e.g. in the High Tech industry) there is only a statistical probability to get the desired output. Another example for the use of this functionality is the expiration of certain products.

The idea for this scenario is a pure sales from stock, i.e. no planned receipts are considered. This is a hard restriction, because planned receipts with CDP-configuration relevance in the make-to-stock segment are not integrated with R/3 (unless IS Mill is used). Figure 7.1 shows the process chain for this scenario.

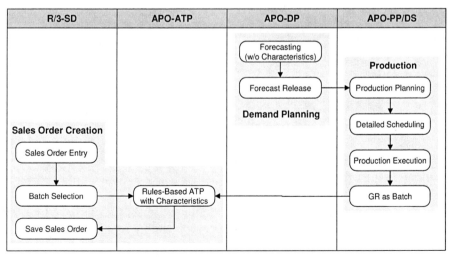

Fig. 7.1. Process Chain for Sales from Stock

The demand planning and the production planning is performed without the consideration of characteristics. The characteristic values are only maintained at goods receipt for the batch. Neither planned orders, production orders nor forecasts have any configuration (unless IS Mill is used).

• *Sales Order Creation*
The sales order receives its requirements for the characteristic via the batch selection. Differing from the usual way of using the batch selection functionality, only the characteristics of the batches are used (and transferred to APO) and not the batch numbers.

• *ATP Check with Characteristics*
Within the ATP check only those elements are used for confirmation which have a configuration that matches the requirements of the sales order. Usually rules-based ATP is used to allow a substitution of the characteristic values (e.g. if multiple values or an interval are maintained as batch selection criteria). This way it is ensured that the sales order has only a single value as requirement (or none if it is not confirmed).

The implication of planning without characteristics is that the scope of the ATP check in the sales order has to be restricted to stock categories. A characteristics value substitution using rules-based ATP is common.

• *Production Planning*
Production planning is performed without the consideration of characteristics. Neither the forecast nor the planned orders have any characteristics as shown in figure 7.2.

CDP_BACON in XX01 (Make-to-stock)										
Avail/Rqmt	Avail/Re...	Category	Receipt/Rqmt. Elemt	Rec/R...	Confir...	Surplu...	C.	P.	C.	N.	M.
28.01.2005 14:30:09	Stock	0000000267/0002/CC	10	10	0	▲			
28.01.2005 14:30:09	Stock	0000000268/0002/CC	10	10	0	▲			
28.01.2005 14:30:09	Stock	0000000278/0002/CC	3	3	0	▲			
28.01.2005 14:30:09	Stock	0000000266/0002/CC	10	10	0	▲			
07.02.2005 00:00:00	PlOrd	1563/0	17	0	0				
07.02.2005 00:00:00	FC req.	1/6893	50-	0	0				

Fig. 7.2. Product View for the Sales from Stock Scenario (APO)

For interactively created planned orders it is possible to maintain a configuration. A pop-up requests the maintenance of a characteristic value, it is however possible to leave the valuation blank.

If many batches with CDP-configuration exist, this might have implications on the performance of the production planning run.

● *Pegging*

With the CDP-configuration scheme supplies are pegged to demands if the valuations of the supplies match the 'requirements' of the demands (or are the same as the valuation of the demand). This behaviour is described in chapter 11 in detail. Demands without 'requirements' or valuations – like the forecast in this scenario – are pegged to supplies of any valuation as shown in figure 7.3.

Pegging Overview For CDP_BACON In XX01 (Make-to-stock)								
Recpt Element	^ R.	Reqmt Element	R.	Receipt Qty	Reqmts Qty	DynPegQty	FixPegQty	ActPegQty
Stock 0000000266/000..	△	FC req. /1/6093		10	50-	10	0	10
Stock 0000000267/000..	△	FC req. /1/6893		10	50-	10	0	10
Stock 0000000268/000..	△	FC req. /1/6893		10	50-	10	0	10
Stock 0000000278/000..	△	FC req. /1/6893		3	50-	3	0	3
PlOrd. 156376		FC req. /1/6893		17	50-	17	0	17

Fig. 7.3. Pegging Overview – Valuated Batches vs. Non-Valuated Requirements

Sales orders without confirmation are another type of demand without 're-quirements'. Since this scenario includes demands without 'requirements' and supplies without valuations, the pegging situation might be rather sub-optimal (as explained in chapter 11) up to not very helpful. The impact of this is that the alert monitor might not be very helpful either.

● *Process Variant: Characteristics in Planning*

In combination with the IS Mill solution it would be possible to use characteristic values in planning as well. In this case CBF would provide forecasts with valuations that would lead to planned orders with valuations – and these are considered for the characteristics based ATP check. Still the scenario has to be a make-to-stock scenario (else neither stock nor planned receipts are considered).

7.1.2 System Configuration Determinants

The material has to be assigned to a batch class (type 023) and the CDP-configuration relevance is required in APO. This scenario makes only sense for a make-to-stock strategy. Because this scenario is independent of production (resp. production is not taken into consideration), it does not matter whether the PDS or the PPM is used.

Requirements Class Account Assignment	Class Type (R/3)	Configuration Scheme	Master Data
Make-to-Stock	Batch (023)	CDP	PPM
Make-to-Order	Variant Config. (300)	VC	PDS

Required / Supported
Supported but Unusual
Not Supported

Fig. 7.4. Determinants for Sales from Stock with Characteristics

If the expiry date is used as a characteristic, all dates should be aggregated e.g. to monthly values (foods is not the target industry). Since each characteristic value requires an own time stream, it is necessary to keep the numbers of characteristic values low in order to keep the performance acceptable.

7.2 Batch Selection in the Sales Order

A different way (than configuration) to assign characteristic values to the sales order is using the batch selection functionality. For this the class type 023 for batches and the CDP-configuration relevance in APO are required. The values of the batch selection are transferred to APO as requirements and not as valuations (differing from the configuration). In APO the ATP check is performed on characteristic level. The characteristic values of the batches that were used for confirmation are used for the sub-items in the R/3 sales order.

● *Value Assignment Before ATP*
The characteristic value assignment is performed using the batch selection. To control that the batch search strategy is carried out before the ATP check and that the values are transferred to APO, an entry in the table TVBX_MAT_CBATP (in R/3) is necessary. This entry is set either via RFC-call if the characteristic view is maintained in APO (see chapter 7.5) or manually.

● *Search Strategy*
The value proposals for the sales order are maintained in the search strategy. Depending on the values of the key fields that are defined in the access sequence (e.g. customer and material), characteristic values are proposed. Figure 7.5 shows the maintenance of the batch search strategy with transaction VCH1.

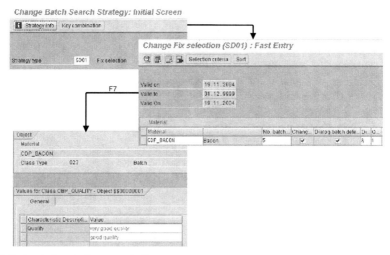

Fig. 7.5. Batch Search Strategy (R/3)

It is either possible to maintain multiple values or an interval – not both (else there will be an error in the integration). Characteristic with optional values should not be used in order to avoid missing requirements.

The search strategy is maintained per strategy type. Figure 7.6 provides an overview about the entities 'access sequence', 'strategy type' and 'search procedure' which are required for the determination of the characteristic values.

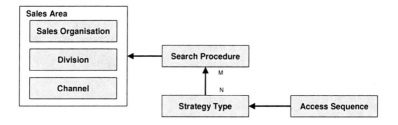

Fig. 7.6. Batch Search Strategy Determination (R/3)

The search procedure is assigned to the sales area via the customising path
Logistics – General → *Batch Management* → *Batch Determination and Batch Check* → *Batch Search Procedure Allocation and Activation* → *Allocate SD Search Procedure/Activate Check*.
The access sequence uses the condition technique and is defined with the customising path

> *Logistics – General* → *Batch Management* → *Batch Determination and Batch Check* → *Access Sequences* → *Define Sales and Distribution Access Sequence*

For the strategy type the customising path is

> *Logistics – General* → *Batch Management* → *Batch Determination and Batch Check* → *Strategy Type* → *Define Sales and Distribution Strategy Type*

and for the search procedure

> ... → *Define Sales and Distribution Search Procedure.*

• *Assignment of Characteristic Values*

The characteristic value assignment is carried out either in the background or as a dialogue depending on the settings in the detail of the search strategy as shown in figure 7.7.

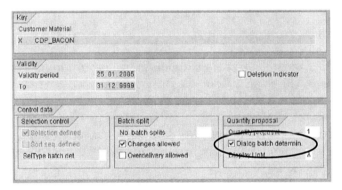

Fig. 7.7. Batch Determination in Background or Dialogue (R/3)

The characteristic value assignment of the sales order is displayed with the icon as shown in figure 7.8.

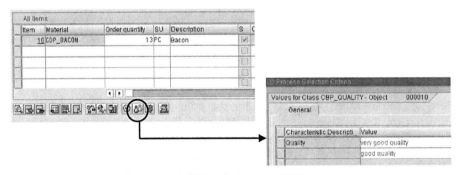

Fig. 7.8. Display Batch Characteristic Value Assignment (R/3)

Make sure that the characteristics are copied into the sales order (and are not just referenced by the strategy). The batch selection characteristic values are transferred as requirements to the sales order in APO as figure 7.9 shows.

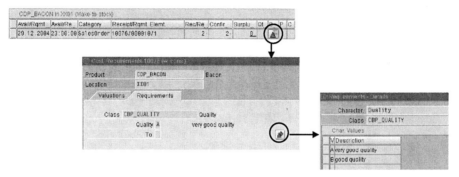

Fig. 7.9. Sales Order with Requirements in APO

In this case a discrete characteristic with multiple valuations without rules-based ATP was used.

7.3 ATP with Characteristics

7.3.1 Characteristic View

As a standard the ATP check (as product check) is carried out on product and location level, optionally on sublocation (i.e. storage location) and version (i.e. batch) level as well. For the ATP with characteristics the ATP check is additionally performed on the level of the characteristic value combination which might have a negative effect on performance.

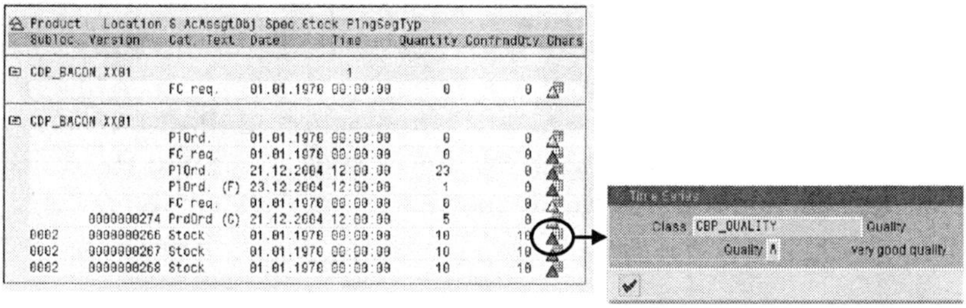

Fig. 7.10. ATP Time Series with Characteristics (APO)

The elements in the ATP time series which have ATP relevant characteristic valuations are displayed with the green triangle as shown in figure 7.10.

ATP with characteristics requires the CDP-configuration relevance and class type 023 for batch classification. The ATP check with characteristics including the rules-based characteristic substitution is only released for SCM 4.1.

• Characteristic View

ATP on characteristics level is activated by the creation of the characteristic view per product and characteristic. Not all characteristics of the class need to be relevant for ATP. The characteristic view is maintained with transaction /SAPAPO/ATPCH01, figure 7.11.

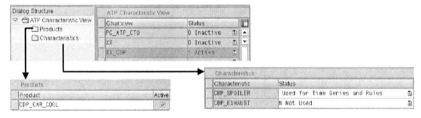

Fig. 7.11. Characteristic View (APO)

• ATP Check with Characteristics

With the activation of the characteristic view the ATP check is performed on characteristic value level, i.e. only the receipts with the same characteristic values are used for the confirmation of the requirement (i.e. sales order). Receipts without characteristic values are regarded as inappropriate for a requirement with characteristic values.

If accidentally no characteristic values are assigned to a requirement it is possible to get an overconfirmation, since the ATP check is carried out on locationproduct, sublocation, batch and characteristic level independently.

7.3.2 Rules-Based ATP with Characteristic Substitution

Within the rules for rules-based ATP (transaction /SAPAPO/RBA04) it is possible to maintain a characteristic substitution procedure (i.e. a list of characteristic values which can be substituted) as shown in figure 7.12.

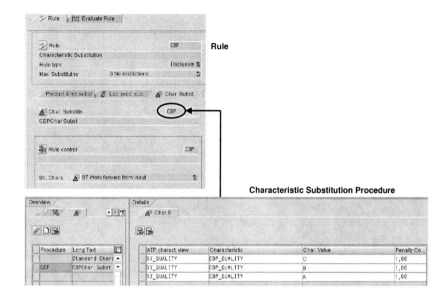

Fig. 7.12. Rules Maintenance for Characteristic Substitution (APO)

The logic for the substitution is the same as with location and product substitution as long as the requirement has only a single characteristic valuation (i.e. no multiple values for the same characteristic).

• *ATP Check with Characteristics*
The ATP check on characteristic level is the special feature within this process. In most cases not only one characteristic value is suitable for a request, therefore rules-based ATP offers the possibility to substitute characteristic values. The result of a rules-based ATP check with characteristic substitution is displayed in figure 7.13.

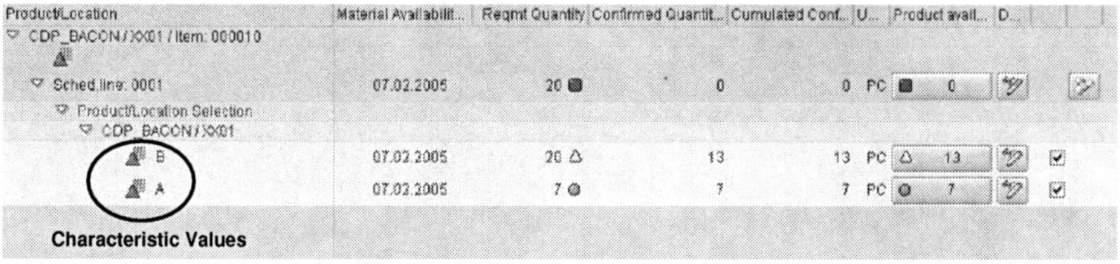

Fig. 7.13. Result of a Rules-Based ATP Check (APO)

In this case the request for 20 pieces was first checked with the lower quality B and for the missing with the higher quality A. Figure 7.14 shows the result of the ATP check in the sales order on R/3-side.

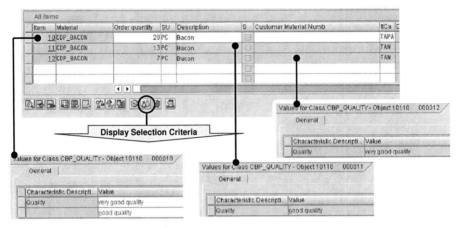

Fig. 7.14. Sales Order in R/3 with Selection Criteria

The two different characteristic values for the confirmation are represented by sub-items. Each of the sub-items has its own configuration (i.e. requirement) according to the result of the ATP check. The item itself has still the initial value resp. values as determined by the selection criteria. In APO only the sub-items are displayed with their confirmed quantities and requirements, figure 7.15.

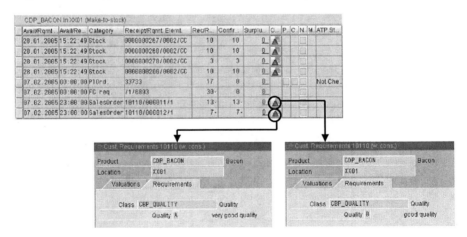

Fig. 7.15. Sales Order in APO

● *Multiple Characteristics*

If multiple characteristics are used the time series are created per characteristic value combination. The batch selection criteria is however still maintained per characteristic, and so is the characteristic substitution procedure within the rules for rules-based ATP.

Rule / Characteristic Substitution Procedure

ATP charact. view	Characteristic	Char. Value	Penalty Co...
XX_PARQUET	CBP_QUALITY	A	1,00
XX_PARQUET	CBP_QUALITY	B	1,00
XX_PARQUET	CBP_BRIGHTNESS	BRIGHT	1,00
XX_PARQUET	CBP_BRIGHTNESS	DARK	1,00

Result of the Rules-Based ATP

Product/Location	Material Availabilit...	Reqmt Quantity	Confirmed Quantit...	Cumulated Conf...	U...	Product avail...	D...
▽ CDP_PARQUET/XX01 / Item: 000010							
▲ /							
▽ Sched line: 0001	21.02.2005	40 ■	0	0	PC	■ 0	📄
▽ Product/Location Selection							
▽ CDP_PARQUET/XX01							
▲ A / BRIGHT	21.02.2005	40 △	10	10	PC	△ 10	📄 ☑
▲ B / BRIGHT	21.02.2005	30 △	5	5	PC	△ 5	📄 ☑
▲ A / DARK	21.02.2005	25 △	20	20	PC	△ 20	📄 ☑
▲ B / DARK	21.02.2005	5 ⊚	5	5	PC	⊚ 5	📄 ☑

Fig. 7.16. Rules-Based ATP with Multiple Characteristic Substitutions.

The consequence is that a controlled substitution of characteristic combinations (e.g. A/BRIGHT or B/DARK) is not possible.

7.4 Delivery with Characteristics

The valuations for the sub-items which have been determined in the rules-based ATP check for the sales order are used for the ATP check in the delivery as well. Since the ATP check in the sales order was already restricted to inventories the probability of a missing availability is comparatively low. In case of a shortage it is however not possible to apply the rules-based ATP in the delivery in order to change the characteristic valuations. For the delivery the same batch search strategy is used as for the sales order. Figure 7.17 shows the delivery with the assigned batches.

All items

Item	Material	Delivery quantity	SU	Description	P...	ItCa	P/V	Batch	Val. Type	Open quantity
10	CDP_BACON	12	PC	Bacon		⊙				13
20	CDP_BACON	7	PC	Bacon		TAN				7

Batch structure for item 10

Item	Material	Delivery quantity	SU	Description	B...	ItCa	P/V	Batch	Val. Type
10	CDP_BACON		PC	Bacon		TAN			
900001	CDP_BACON	10	PC	Bacon		TAN	A	0000000267	
900002	CDP_BACON	2	PC	Bacon		TAN	A	0000000278	

Fig. 7.17. Delivery (R/3)

The delivery is transferred to APO, as shown in figure 7.18.

CDP_BACON in XX01 (Make-to-stock)											
Avail/Rqmt	Avail/Re	Category	Receipt/Rqmt. Elemt.	Rec/R.	Confir.	Surplu	Qt.	C.	P.	C.	N.	M.
11.03.2005	13:46.17	Stock	0000000267/0002/CC	10	10	0		▲			
11.03.2005	13:46.17	Stock	0000000268/0002/CC	10	10	10	🔳	▲			
11.03.2005	13:46.17	Stock	0000000278/0002/CC	2	2	0		▲			
11.03.2005	13:46.17	Stock	0000000266/0002/CC	10	10	3	🔳	▲			
11.03.2005	00:00:00	Deliv.	80013388/900001	10-	10-	0		▲			
11.03.2005	00:00:00	Deliv.	80013388/900002	2-	2-	0		▲			
11.03.2005	00:00:00	Deliv.	80013388/900003	7-	7-	0		▲			

Fig. 7.18. Delivery in APO

For each batch split a separate line with its own requirement is created.

8 Configure-to-Order with Propagation

8.1 Scenario Description

8.1.1 Process Chain

The specific feature of the scenario 'configure-to-order with propagation' is that it is a make-to-order process for the finished product and a make-to-stock process for the assembly groups. Additionally the assembly groups have characteristics which are propagated from the finished product and are usually handled in batches. Figure 8.1 shows the process chain for the scenario 'configure-to-order with propagation'.

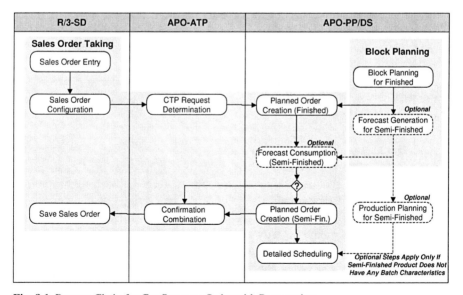

Fig. 8.1. Process Chain for Configure-to-Order with Propagation

This scenario is mainly used for the mill industries. The mill industries is a collective term for the metal, the paper, the wood, the textile and the foil industries. The peculiarity in those areas is that the material flow is divergent from the key material – e.g. the steel coil or the paper reel. These key materials have usually a long lead time and are handled in (huge) batches. The finished products are usually produced as make-to-order, and the availability is frequently restricted by the inventory of the key material and the capacity of the key resources. The key material is often produced in-house but might be externally procured as well. In many of the industries – e.g. the steel industry – the key materials have batch characteristics to describe their grade, thickness, length and other properties which are usually only known at the time of the goods receipt. An example for these are steel coils. On the other hand the requirements for the key component cover a range of properties and therefore it is usually possible to use key components of different properties for the same finished product. In this case the 'requirements' (as a property within CDP, see also chapter 11) of the dependent demand are applied to select an appropriate batch.

Depending whether the components have batch characteristics or not, the optional steps can be applied. For components with batch characteristics they do not make any sense. The scenario relies on the CTP check in the sales order which triggers the production. Often block planning is used to provide a rough cut scheduling for the planned orders, but it is neither mandatory for this scenario to use block planning nor is block planning restricted to this scenario. In this case we assume that the block planning takes place on the finished product level – depending on the production requirements it might be any other level as well. A subsequent detailed scheduling step is mandatory.

For the integration of the valuated planned and production orders into the make-to-stock segment for the key components the IS Mill solution is required on R/3 side.

• Assignment of Characteristic Values
The configuration of the sales order is performed as described in chapter 5. For most cases this is sufficient, for others (e.g. cables) additionally a batch selection as described in chapter 7 can be carried out if requirements are needed for the sales order – e.g. because the consideration of appropriate batches takes place already on finished product level. Another case is the modelling of tolerances (e.g. for the thickness of steel sheets) as requirements. In these cases the variant configuration must be compatible with the batch selection (i.e. the valuation must be within the requirements) to avoid errors in further processing.

● *Production Planning & Characteristic Propagation*

The most common characteristic-related property of the planned order for the finished product is the propagation of characteristic values from the finished product to the dependent demand. For the PPMs this functionality has to be configured explicitely, for the PDS the propagation of a characteristic value is performed as a default. If the characteristic value has to be manipulated (e.g. if the finished product is 'RED', the component should be 'BLUE'), object dependencies as described in chapter 5 have to be used.

● *Requirements for the Dependent Demand with the PDS*

For some business cases it is necessary to use requirements for the characteristic values in the dependent demand (e.g. cables because the length is modelled as a characteristic). Using the PPM it is possible to define requirements for characteristic values. With APO 4.1 this is not possible within the PDS. There is however a way to model requirements when planning with the PDS as well by defining the requirements for the planned order directly (instead of defining it in the PDS). For this purpose the BAdI /SAPAPO/RRP_SRC_EXIT for the planned order creation has to be used. The method RRP_USEX_PLORD_CREATE allows the definition and assignment of the requirements.

If planning is performed with requirements, specific production planning heuristics are required. The normal production planning heuristic does not provide sufficient results.

● *Optional: Planning for Semi-Finished Using Block Planning*

In some cases – e.g. for paper industry – the key component (the pulp) does not necessarily have any batch characteristics. In combination with block planning it is possible to create independent requirements for these components based on the blocks. The optional steps cover this case.

8.1.2 System Configuration Determinants

As soon as batch characteristic are used, the CDP-class system is mandatory. Since APO was used for mill industries before the PDS master data object existed, both PPM and PDS can be used in this case. It is however recommended to use the PDS for new implementations because the PPM will not be developed any further. If the PPM is used, the logic for the processing of the characteristic values has to be maintained within the PPMs on APO side. Figure 8.2 provides an overview about the settings.

Requirements Class Account Assignment	Class Type (R/3)	Configuration Scheme	Master Data
Make-to-Stock	Batch (023)	CDP	PPM
Make-to-Order	Variant Config. (300)	VC	PDS

Required / Supported
Supported but Unusual
Not Supported

Fig. 8.2. Determinants for Configure-to-Order with Propagation

Usually a make-to-order requirements strategy is used for the finished product and make-to-stock for the key components. In some cases a make-to-stock strategy is used for the finished product as well, and the sales order is connected with the receipt by compatible characteristic values. Since the CDP-configuration scheme is used, all elements have their own valuations. For the assignment of the valuation to the sales order the finished product must be configurable and classes of both types (300 and 023) have to be assigned to the material master in R/3. Both classes must contain the same APO relevant characteristics. Figure 8.3 shows the product master in APO with the classes of the types 300 and 400.

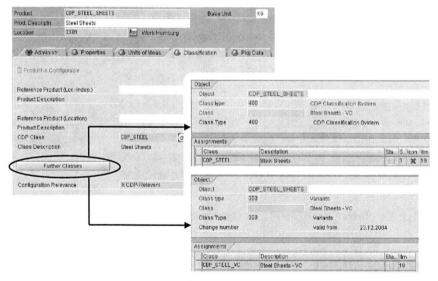

Fig. 8.3. Class Assignment for the Finished Product (APO)

Another important prerequisite is the use of the IS Mill solution on R/3-side in order to allow planned resp. production orders for the semi-finished products with valuation but without a sales order assignment.

8.2 Characteristic Propagation within the PPM

The propagation of characteristics is possible with both the PDS and the PPM. For the PDS this is already explained in chapter 5. Historically the characteristic propagation as described in this chapter was developed and used for mill industries. Currently this is the only scenario where characteristics propagation within the PPM is used – the use of the PDS is recommended for new implementations. For new implementations the PDS normally covers the requirements for the scenario with the advantage of improved R/3-integration. Characteristic propagation in the PPM is only possible for the CDP-configuration relevance.

Due to the divergent material flow, in the mill industries stock is usually kept for the raw material (e.g. the steel coil or the paper reel), which is used to produce many different products. The finished product is usually produced for the individual sales order. Therefore one of the key functions is to propagate the valuations of the sales order to the dependent demand of the planned resp. the production order.

The settings for the propagation of the valuations are maintained within the PPM with the transaction /SAPAPO/SCC05. The maintenance for the characteristic propagation settings is activated with the menu path *plan → characteristics propagation → use* and changed with the menu path *goto → characteristic propagation: overview* as shown in figure 8.4.

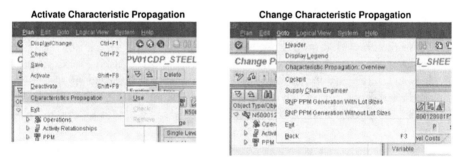

Fig. 8.4. Activate and Change the Characteristic Propagation in the PPM (APO)

The entry screen for the characteristic propagation maintenance provides an overview about the input and output products and which classes are assigned to the products or to the operation, the activity or the plan itself.

D..	Component	Classification	O.	Description	
	N500012890IPV01.			Steel Sheets	
	CDP_STEEL_SHE..	CBP_STEEL		CDP_STEEL_SHEETS / P / 00	
	CDP_STEEL_COIL	CBP_STEEL		CDP_STEEL_COILS M00002	
	001000000001			001000000001	
	P			P / 001000000001	

Fig. 8.5. Characteristic Propagation Maintenance Screen in the PPM (APO)

The classification is set by default for all classified products and block-planned activities (the product and the resource master are checked for reasonable proposals). If components are added later, the class proposal has to be triggered interactively within the characteristic propagation maintenance screen with the menu path *propagation → propose classes*. It is possible to use the classification additionally on plan and on operation level to change settings according to the valuations.

It is possible to assign a class interactively to any of these levels. In this case the flag 'only rules/parameters' is set automatically. This flag controls that the characteristic values are only used for the rules but no characteristic values will be adopted to the planned order. Therefore, if a class assignment is expected but does not show, check the master data instead of maintaining it interactively.

For the classified output product the standard valuation and the standard requirements are defined. The standard valuation is used if the demand does not have any valuation, and the standard requirement of the output product defines for which valuation the PPM might be used. Figure 8.6 shows the principle of the characteristic propagation from the valuation of the output node to the valuation of the input node.

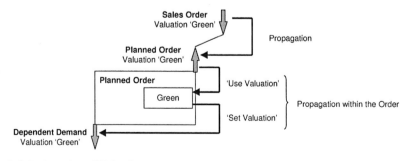

Fig. 8.6. Propagation of Valuations

For the propagation of the valuations of the output product to the components, on the output product level the flag 'use valuation' has to be set in the 'valuations'-view and on the component level the according flag 'set valuation' has to be set as shown in figure 8.7.

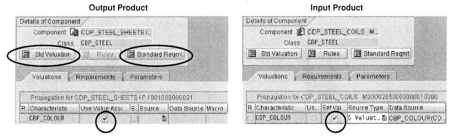

Fig. 8.7. Required Setting for Characteristic Propagation (APO)

The standard requirements for the output product are used as a selection criterion for the PPM – i.e. to cover a demand, the valuation of the demand must match the requirements of the output product.

In this case the valuation is propagated with the same value. It is however also possible to apply a more complex logic using macros. The requirements for the component are maintained as standard requirements. It is also possible to change the requirements depending on the valuation of the output product, e.g. with the use of macros. These macros have to be created in APO, no integration with the object dependencies from R/3 is possible. Requirements set in macros must be kept compatible with the valuations without system support. This functionality originates from APO 3.x when requirements were mandatory for pegging. With APO 4.1 this should only be used in exceptional cases.

• *Characteristics as Selection Criteria*
Characteristic value can be applied in the PPM to perform a selection of the component, the mode (i.e. the resource) and the set-up group. The logic is quite similar for all of these selections. Therefore only the selection of the set-up group is explained in detail. In the example shown in figure 8.8 the set-up group XX1 is selected if the value of the operation is 'GREEN' and the set-up group XX2 if the value is 'RED'.

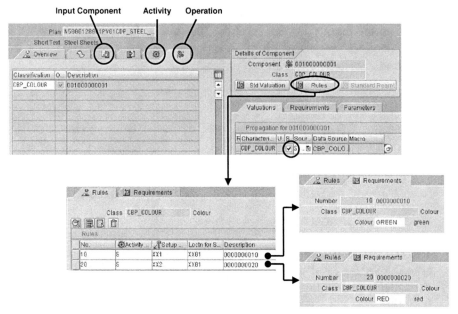

Fig. 8.8. Characteristic Based Set-Up Group Determination (APO)

The logic for the selection is maintained as rules on operation level. The rule itself is an identifier which combines the object to which it relates (in this case the activity of the type 'S') with the set-up group. The selection conditions are maintained as 'requirements' in the details of the rule.

The selection of components and modes is performed analogously on the input material level resp. the activity level.

8.3 Block Planning

8.3.1 Motivation for Block Planning

The idea of block planning is to reserve capacity on key resources for orders with certain properties. Especially in the mill industries the valuation of the output product might have a significant impact on the production – for instance for the coating of steel the type of the coating is substantial for the production planning, since the effort for the set-up between different coatings is considerable. Other examples are the paper production that must use up a large amount of pulp or steel processing where huge quantities have to be processed within a short time (e.g. due to solidification).

The sequence of the pulp or steel qualities – the cycles – can be roughly planned or is known from experience. Since the sales orders and – in the make-to-order environment – the planned orders are not yet available, with block planning the resource capacity is reserved for certain characteristic values of the operations. The length of these blocks are defined by the planner, often using a reference cycle and adjusted interactively.

8.3.2 Block Definition in the Resource

For block planning a class of the type 400 (R/3: 300 or 023) in APO is required. This class needs to contain the relevant characteristic or characteristics and is assigned to the resource master (model independently). Within R/3 only the characteristics are required, the class can be defined in APO if no meaningful class can be integrated. The blocks themselves are defined version dependently, figure 8.9.

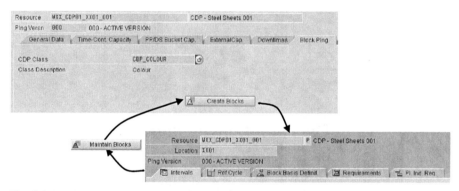

Fig. 8.9. Block Definition in the Resource (APO)

The intervals are the blocks and define the requirements of the resource for a time interval. The block basis definitions are the identifiers for the requirement of a block. These are either directly or via a reference cycle assigned to the intervals as shown in figure 8.10. The use of reference cycles is common but optional.

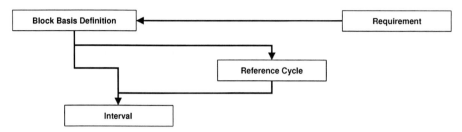

Fig. 8.10. Entities for the Block Maintenance

The block basis definitions including the requirements and the reference cycles are resource independent, i.e. they can be used for all resources with the same class. Figure 8.11 shows the screens for the maintenance of the rules resp. block basis definition and the reference cycle.

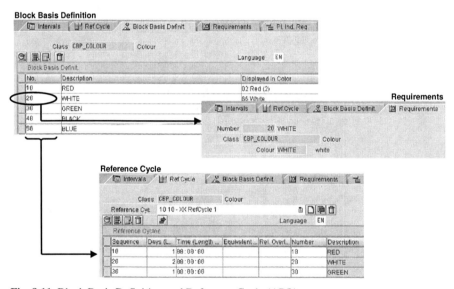

Fig. 8.11. Block Basis Definition and Reference Cycle (APO)

The blocks are defined by the assignment of the block basis definitions and/or the reference cycles to the intervals, figure 8.12.

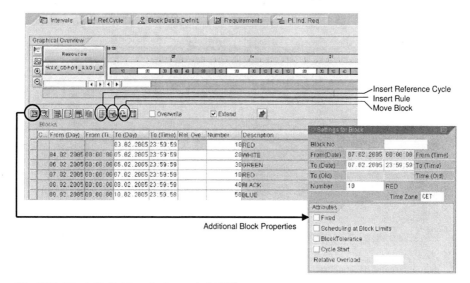

Fig. 8.12. Block Definition via Intervals (APO)

In the 'intervals'-view additional properties of the blocks are maintained, e.g. a fixing of the block, whether the scheduling has to be performed at the block limits and block tolerances (i.e. how much an activity might exceed the block limits). The fixing of the block causes that no planning into the block is allowed and the activities inside the block are not scheduled any more (though the activities do not have the status 'fixed'). The block sizes are changed either by overwriting the dates of the blocks or via drag and drop in the graphical overview (see figure 8.12). Block planning can not be used for secondary resources.

• *Visualisation of the Blocks in the Planning Board*
The blocks are displayed per default as thin lines within the resource. With a set-get parameter in the user settings (/SAPAPO/CDPS_BLOCK = 1) it is possible to change the display of the blocks to boxes. The colour of these lines is defined in the maintenance for the rules resp. block basic definitions.

Resources Chart												
Resource	6.02.2006	07.02.2006	08.02.2006	09.02.2006	10.02.2006	11.02.2006	12.02.2005	13.02.2006	14.02.2005	15.02.2006	16.02.2005	17.02.2005	18.02.2005
WXX_CDP01												

Fig. 8.13. Block Planning in the Planning Board (APO)

With right mouse click on the blocks it is possible to branch into the block maintenance. An extended block maintenance is possible by calling the heuristic SAP_CDPBP_03 from the planning board.

Period from	07.02.2005	00:00:00	To	31.12.2007	23:59:49		
Maint. Mode	TD Productive Time (Delta)		Changed Blocks		Subsequent Blocks		
			● Extend		● Move All		
			○ Move		○ Move Selected Blocks		

From (Day)	From (Ti...	To (Day)	To (Time)	Net Capacit...	Delta [	Committed ...	Free Capacity [	Utiliza...	Rule...	Rule Description	Fix	R...	Tolera...
07.02.20...	00:00:00	07.02.2005	23:59:59	24:00:00	0,00		24:00:00	0,00	10	RED			0
08.02.2005	00:00:00	08.02.2005	23:59:59	24:00:00	0,00	9:59:59	14:00:01	41,67	40	BLACK			0
08.02.2005	00:00:00	10.02.2005	23:59:58	47:58:59	0,00	9:59:59	38:00:00	20,83	50	BLUE			0
10.02.2005	23:59:59	11.02.2005	23:59:58	24:00:00	0,00	9:59:59	14:00:01	41,67	10	RED			0
11.02.2005	23:59:59	13.02.2005	23:59:58	0:00:02	0,00		0:00:02	0,00	20	WHITE			0
13.02.2005	23:59:59	14.02.2005	23:59:59	23:59:59	0,00	17:00:00	6:59:59	70,83	30	GREEN			0
14.02.2005	23:59:59	15.02.2005	23:59:58	24:00:00	0,00		24:00:00	0,00	10	RED			0

Fig. 8.14. Extended Block Planning (APO)

As a prerequisite the heuristic SAP_CDPBP_03 has to be assigned to the heuristic profile of the planning board.

8.3.3 Activity Valuation

The principle of the block planning functionality is to define requirements for the blocks on the resource and to valuate the activities. The definition of the requirements for the blocks is quite independent of the scenario, but how to valuate the activities depends on the master data (PDS or PPM) and whether the product is configurable or not. For the use of PPMs the CDP-configuration scheme is required, for PDS both VC- and CDP-configuration scheme are supported (with APO 4.1).

• *Valuation of Activities via Characteristic Propagation in the PPM*
For a configurable product we do have a valuation at the demand node (usually the sales order) which will cause a valuation of the supply node of the planned order. To propagate the valuation of the output product to the activity, the activity has to be classified in the characteristic propagation settings within the PPM and the flag 'set valuation' must be set, figure 8.15. The class of the activity has to contain the characteristic that is used for block planning. Make sure that the indicator for 'only rules/ parameters' is initial (otherwise the activity will not be valuated).

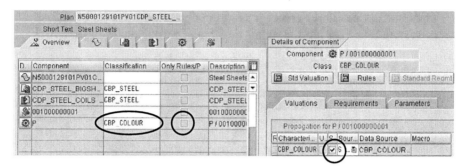

Fig. 8.15. Valuation of the Activity (APO)

Again it is possible to apply a more complex logic for the propagation using macros. The rules (the button in the top right area) can be used for the selection of modes within the activity, e.g. to exclude modes for certain values of the characteristic. All of these definitions have to be maintained manually in APO.

If the demand node does not have any valuation – i.e. if the product of the master output is not CDP-configuration relevant – it is possible to define a standard valuation for the activity. In this case block planning is not carried out according to the configuration resp. the valuation of the finished product but according to the product itself (or to be more precise: the PPM). For simple cases with fix valuation (i.e. no characteristic propagation, just standard valuation) it is possible to set these values during the CIF transfer as described in note 495825.

● *Valuation of Activities via Object Dependencies*
With the PDS the activity is valuated per default with the characteristic values of the order resp. the output node if the resource is relevant for block planning. Neither class assignment nor object dependencies are required for this. If a more complex logic is required – e.g. to set the value of the block planning characteristic depending on the value of another characteristic – object dependencies (procedures) have to be used. These object dependencies must be assigned to the dependency group SAPAPOACT. This dependency group is used to control that the object dependency is assigned to the activity (and not to the operation or the mode, see chapter 5). As an example the value of the characteristic CBP_COLOUR (which is used for block planning) for the activity is set to 'BLACK' if the value of the quality for the order is 'A':

```
$SELF.CDP_COLOUR = 'BLACK' if $ROOT.CBP_QUALITY = 'A'.
```

The object dependency is assigned to the operation within the routing. The corresponding PDS has the object dependency assigned to the activity.

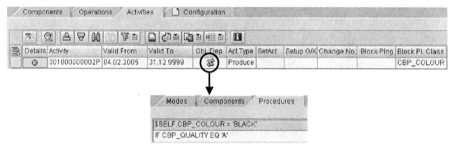

Fig. 8.16. Object Dependencies in the PDS (APO)

If block planning is to be used for non-configurable products, a fix valuation has to be assigned to the operation of the routing in R/3. For this purpose a class of type 018 has to be created and assigned to the operation (with the path *extras* → *classification* → *operations* within the routing) as shown in figure 8.17.

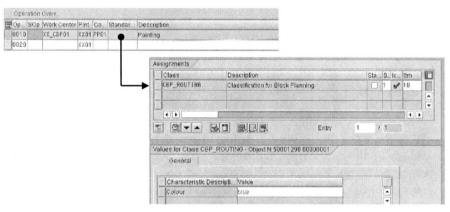

Fig. 8.17. Valuation of the Operation for Non-Configurable Materials (R/3)

The class has to contain the characteristic that is used for block planning. No additional class transfer to APO is required. However, to transfer the valuation to APO the method USE_OPERATION_CLASSIFICATION of the BAdI CUSLNTRTO_ADDIN on R/3-side has to be implemented (by adding the coding line EV_TRUE = 'X'.) and activated.

The valuation of the operation is displayed in the PDS with transaction /SAPAPO/CURTO_SIMU as shown in figure 8.18 in the details of the block planning indicator.

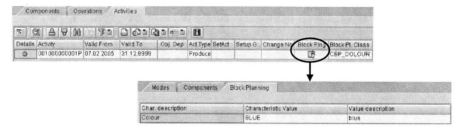

Fig. 8.18. Valuation of the Activity for Non-Configurable Products in the PDS (APO)

Note that the block planning class is the class of the resource in APO and not the class of the routing in R/3. The block planning settings for the resource have to be maintained before integrating the PDS to APO.

Per default only the activities of the type 'production' are valuated. If it is required to valuate the set-up activities as well, this must be done via BAdI. For this purpose the method BLOCK_PLANNING_RELEVANCE of the BAdI /SAPAPO/CURTO_CREATE has to be implemented.

8.3.3 Block Planning Functions

Block planning was originally developed for the need of the mill industries but is used by other industries as well – both for configurable and for non-configurable products. Note 528189 describes the block planning specific scheduling options (planning at the block limits, fixing of blocks) and gives additional information about the properties and limitations.

8.3.4 Assembly Planning Based on Block Definitions

Usually the production strategy in the mill industries is only make-to-order for the finished product and make-to-stock for the key assembly groups. The planning for the assembly groups might be performed consumption based or via forecast. The functionality described in this chapter offers a help for the generation of the forecast.

The generation of forecasts based on the block definitions in block planning makes only sense if the input material is neither configurable nor subject to planning relevant batch characteristics. The forecast is generated for the input material of the products which use the block planning. The basis for this is the PDS resp. the PPM of the product which is produced on the resource. Either one product per resource or one product per block is specified to provide the relation between productive time and base quantity. This specification is maintained in the 'planned independent requirement'-view of the block definitions within the resource, figure 8.19.

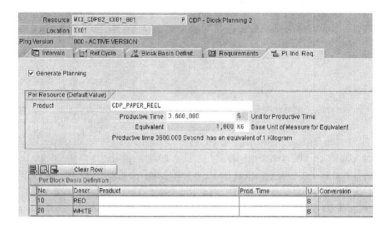

Fig. 8.19. Settings for the Forecast Generation Within the Block of the Resource (APO)

The quantity for the forecast is calculated using the PDS resp. PPM of the specified product. Note that in the PDS selection conditions resp. in the PPM rules have to exist for all the requirement values of the blocks else the forecast generation terminates with an error. For example, if one block has a requirement that includes 'RED' and 'ORANGE', both for 'RED' and 'ORANGE' selection conditions resp. rules have to exist. The forecast generation itself is called with the transaction /SAPAPO/BLRG01. Figure 8.20 shows the result screen.

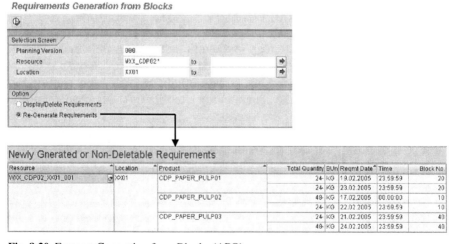

Fig. 8.20. Forecast Generation from Blocks (APO)

The forecast generation does not support any characteristics. Though it is possible to enhance the forecast with characteristics using the BAdI /SAPAPO/BLRG_BADI_EX, the forecast consumption for dependent demand does not consider characteristics in any way.

8.4 Goods Receipt with Batch Characteristics

If a batch class is assigned to the material master and the checkbox for batch management in the 'work scheduling'-view is selected, batch numbers are created for each goods receipt and the valuation of the batch is requested via pop-up as shown in figure 8.21.

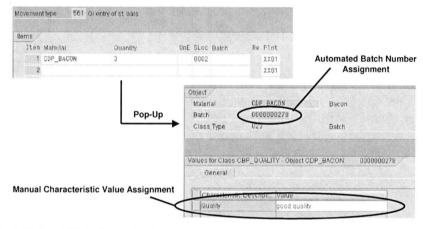

Fig. 8.21. Batch Valuation at Goods Receipt (R/3)

The batches and their valuations are transferred to APO (if the transfer of batches is active in the CIF model) as shown in the product view in figure 8.22.

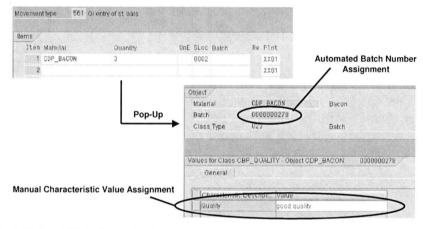

Fig. 8.22. Batches with Characteristics in APO

For the use of batch characteristics in APO the CDP-configuration relevance is mandatory.

The 'version'-view of the product view provides a more detailed overview about the batches and their valuations, figure 8.23.

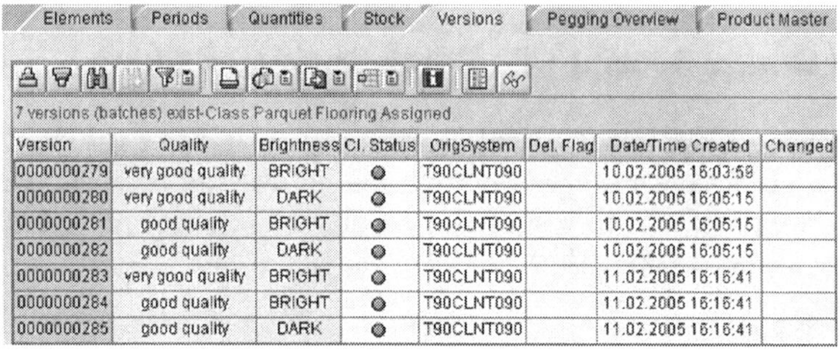

Version	Quality	Brightness	Cl. Status	OrigSystem	Del. Flag	Date/Time Created	Changed
0000000279	very good quality	BRIGHT	◉	T90CLNT090		10.02.2005 16:03:59	
0000000280	very good quality	DARK	◉	T90CLNT090		10.02.2005 16:05:15	
0000000281	good quality	BRIGHT	◉	T90CLNT090		10.02.2005 16:05:15	
0000000282	good quality	DARK	◉	T90CLNT090		10.02.2005 16:05:15	
0000000283	very good quality	BRIGHT	◉	T90CLNT090		11.02.2005 16:16:41	
0000000284	good quality	BRIGHT	◉	T90CLNT090		11.02.2005 16:16:41	
0000000285	good quality	DARK	◉	T90CLNT090		11.02.2005 16:16:41	

Fig. 8.23. Version View of the Product View (APO)

• *Deactivation of Batches*
Since batches are a different entity than inventory and the batches still exist even when the inventory has been issued long ago, it is necessary to deactivate batches that are not needed any more with the report RVBDEACT (or to archive the batches in R/3) in order to ensure system performance.

9 Planning with Shelf Life

9.1 Scenario Description

9.1.1 Process Chain

The planning with shelf life is mainly relevant for industries with perishable products and a make-to-stock production – e.g. foods and pharma. In these cases planning has to ensure that the products still have a certain shelf life at their demand date.

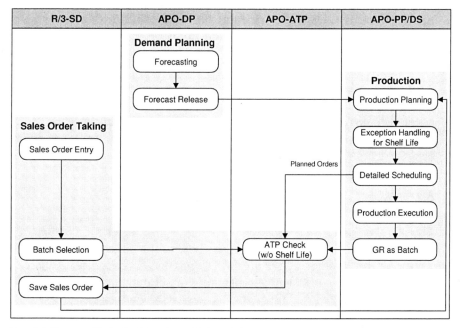

Fig. 9.1. Process Chain for Planning with Shelf Life

Since shelf life planning in APO is limited to the locationproduct-level, in a straightforward model the shelf life limitations will be lost with each production step and each stock transfer. Nevertheless it is often possible to limit the shelf life planning problem to one critical locationproduct and use customer reports to identify possible problems on other levels and treat these as exceptions. In the following we assume that the shelf life problem for planning is limited to one locationproduct only. Figure 9.1 shows a sample process for the shelf life scenario.

Demand planning is performed assuming that the shelf life requirements will be met – i.e. without any consideration of the shelf life. The main specific of the process is that the shelf life restrictions are considered in production planning and scheduling. The sales order might transfer a customer specific shelf life requirement, but the shelf life is not considered in the ATP check.

● *ATP Check*

It is not possible with standard ATP methods to take the shelf life information into account for the ATP check – neither with the ATP time series nor with the ATP check within the pegging network (the setting 'characteristic evaluation' in the check mode).

A possible solution on customer project basis might be to enhance the ABAP class for CTP and to perform the ATP check within the pegging network. Other ATP functions as 'full delivery' might violate the constraints nevertheless.

● *Alternative Approach: Reporting*

In some cases the problem of expiring inventories can be solved as well by a report to list the batches which are expired or will expire soon. If the shelf life is long compared to the planning horizon, this approach should be considered as an alternative.

9.1.2 System Configuration Determinants

The prerequisite for the use of shelf life are batch characteristics (type 023) in R/3. The shelf life functionality does not require any configuration relevance for the product. Therefore this scenario is independent of the configuration scheme, but shelf life planning is not compatible with the VC-configuration relevance (i.e. if the VC-configuration scheme is used, the product must not be configurable). The indicator for shelf life planning has to be set in the product master as well.

Shelf life planning is usually only applied in a make-to-stock environment, though it would be technically possible to use it with a make-to-order strategy as well. The shelf life functionality is independent of the master data object – i.e. both the PDS and the PPM can be used.

Requirements Class Account Assignment	Class Type (R/3)	Configuration Scheme	Master Data
Make-to-Stock	Batch (023)	CDP	PPM
Make-to-Order	Variant Config. (300)	VC	PDS

Required / Supported
Supported but Unusual
Not Supported

Fig. 9.2. Determinants for Shelf Life Planning

9.1.3 Shelf Life Settings in the Material Master

In the material master the indicator for batch management has to be set and the shelf life data in the 'plant data / storage 1' view needs to be maintained.

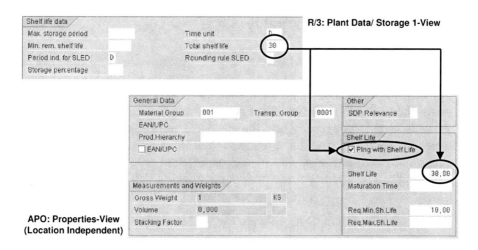

Fig. 9.3. Material Master Settings for Shelf Life

The value for the total shelf life is transferred from the R/3 material master to the APO product master and triggers the setting for 'planning with shelf life'. Note that this information is location independent in APO. The required minimum shelf life and – if needed – the required maximum shelf life have to be maintained manually resp. via user-exit.

Since APO 4.0 it is possible to plan with location dependent shelf life data as well. The flag 'planning with shelf life' triggers that shelf life data is displayed on the location dependent demand view of the product, figure 9.4.

Fig. 9.4. Location Dependent Shelf Life in the 'Demand'-View of the Product Master

Additionally the classes and characteristics for shelf life have to be assigned to the material master in R/3, see chapter 9.3. The assignment is neither required in APO nor is it transferred to the product master.

Characteristics are only required for the integration of the batch information from R/3. Apart from this the shelf life planning is not based on characteristics (neither technically nor in display – the shelf life information is stored differently in live cache and the products are not configuration relevant, though a batch class is assigned in R/3.

9.2 Shelf Life Functionality

Especially in foods industries, but in other businesses as well (pharmaceutical industries for instance) shelf life is an issue which needs to be considered in planning. The shelf life functionality in APO covers two aspects of this, the shelf life itself (i.e. the expiration) and the maturity. This information is used in pegging, where the shelf life and the maturity of a supply element are checked with the required shelf life and – optionally – with the required maximum shelf life of a demand element. Figure 9.5 illustrates this logic. The additional constraints for pegging defined by the shelf life function are

$$\text{Rqmt. Date} \geq \text{Avail. Date} + \text{Maturity} \tag{9.1}$$

$$\text{Rqmt. Date} + \text{Req. Max Shelf Life} \geq \text{Avail. Date} + \text{Shelf Life} \tag{9.2}$$

$$\text{Rqmt. Date} + \text{Req. Min Shelf Life} \leq \text{Avail. Date} + \text{Shelf Life} \tag{9.3}$$

In the first case in figure 9.5 the constraint in formula 9.1 (and 9.2) is violated, in case 2 constraint 9.2 and in case 4 constraint 9.3.

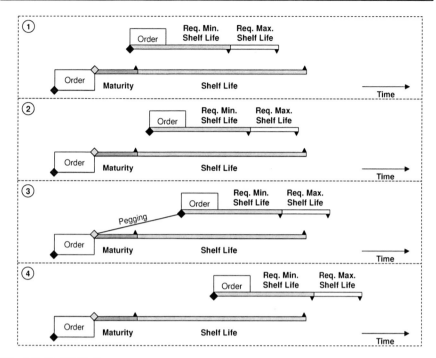

Fig. 9.5. Shelf Life Dates

Shelf life is activated by setting the according flag in the 'attributes' view of the product master. The durations for maturity, shelf life, required shelf life and required maximum shelf life are maintained in the 'attributes' view as described in 9.1.3.

The information regarding shelf life is displayed in the product view, if shelf life is activated. Figure 9.6 shows the product view for an example as in figure 9.5.

Receipt	Maturity	Shelf Life
Requirement	Required Min. Shelf Life	Required Max. Shelf Life

Rqts/avail. date	Rqts/av.	Category	Receipt/rqmt. elemt.	Rec./issue qty	Surplus/shortfall	Qty alert	MtyReq SLDate	ReqMaxSLDate
26.04.2003	23:59:59		End of production...					
30.04.2003	22:00:00	PlOrd. (F)	33562	100	75		10.05.2003	29.06.2003
05.05.2003	12:00:00	FC req		25-	25-		04.06.2003	14.06.2003
15.05.2003	12:00:00	FC req		25-	25-		14.06.2003	24.06.2003
30.05.2003	12:00:00	FC req		25-	0		29.06.2003	09.07.2003
15.06.2003	12:00:00	FC req		25-	25-		15.07.2003	25.07.2003

Fig. 9.6. Display of Shelf Life Information in Product View (APO)

The difference between shelf life and a maximum pegging constraint is that the goods receipt date of the batches is taken into account, i.e. the maturity and the shelf life are adjusted with proceeding time, figure 9.7.

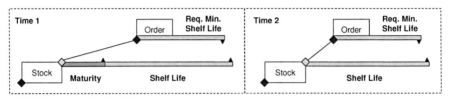

Fig. 9.7. Adjustment of the Shelf Life with Time

9.3 Characteristics for Shelf Life

Characteristics and object dependencies are mainly required to store the shelf life and the maturity of batches. A second usage is the transfer of customer specific required shelf life.

• Characteristics and Classes for Shelf Life
For shelf life a class of type 023 is required. As described in the notes 391018 and 751392 this class should contain the following standard characteristics
  • LOBM_VERAB
  • LOBM_VFDAT
  • LOBM_HSDAT.
The characteristic LOBM_HSDAT has to be created according to note 394229 as shown in figure 9.8 (for R/3 4.7 create only the characteristic and do not carry out any of the other actions).

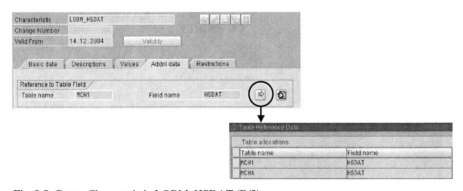

Fig. 9.8. Create Characteristic LOBM_HSDAT (R/3)

Additionally the new characteristics

- LOBM_APO_SL_MIN: Min. shelf life/maturity in sec., type NUM 15,3
- LOBM_APO_SL_MAX: Max. shelf life/maturity in sec., type NUM 15,3
- LOBM_APO_SL_UTC: Reference time stamp, type NUM 15,0.

have to be created and assigned to the class. These characteristics should have the flag 'not ready for input' and 'no display'. The naming convention of the new characteristics is essential. These characteristics are either explicitly created or with the report Z_ADD_LOBM_APO_SL_CHARS as in note 602174. After the report has run, the characteristics have to be updated from client 000 with transaction BMSM.

If configured materials are used together with shelf life, additionally the characteristics SL_MIN_DAYS, SL_MIN_DAYS2, SL_MAX_DAYS and SL_MAX_DAYS2 have to be created and assigned to the variant configuration class (type 300) to transfer the shelf life requirements as explained in note 391018. Only the new characteristics have to be transferred to APO, e.g. by assigning the organisational area only to the new characteristics only as shown in figure 9.9.

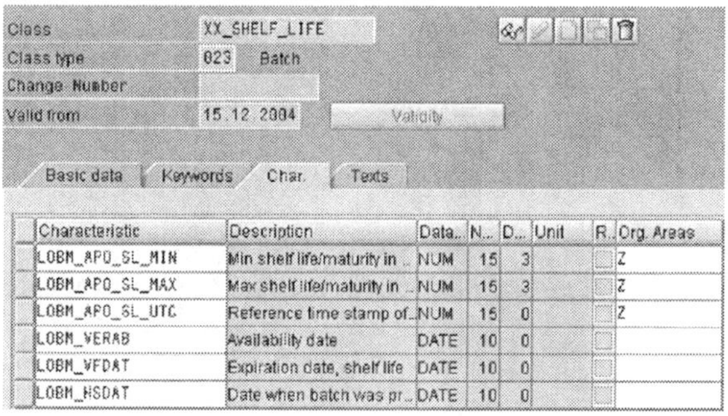

Fig. 9.9. Class for Shelf Life (R/3)

For some of the characteristics object dependencies are required as described in note 391018. These are created either interactively or with transaction BMSM as well – provided that no object dependencies exist already. The old object dependencies are deleted either manually or with the report Z_DEL_SL_OBJECT_DEPS as described in note 604757.

- *Transfer of Characteristics and Classes to APO*

Different from the other cases, the characteristics LOBM_APO_SL_MIN, LOBM_APO_SL_MAX and LOBM_APO_SL_UTC are only assigned to the class type 230 in APO and not to the class type 400 (nor is it possible to assign these characteristics to the class type 400). Differing from R/3, no class is assigned to the product and the configuration relevance indicator is set to 'not relevant for configuration'.

Make sure that the indicator for material configuration is not set in the 'basic data 2'-view (unless configuration is used for another purpose – in this case the VC-configuration scheme is not compatible with the shelf life functionality).

• Characteristic Customising in APO
For the display of the shelf life relevant data of the batches it is necessary that the organisational area of the characteristics LOBM_APO_SL_MIN, LOBM_APO_SL_MAX and LOBM_APO_SL_UTC is assigned to the class types 230 (all organisational areas should be maintained in APO). This assignment is possible with transaction O1CL analogous as described in chapter 3 and shown in figure 9.10.

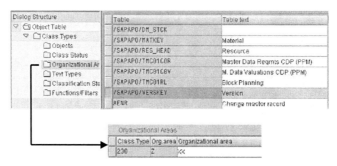

Fig. 9.10. Assignment of Organisational Areas to Class Type for Batches (APO)

• Re-Evaluation of Batches
If batches already exist before the configuration of the shelf life settings (resp. before the change of the classes), the batches need to be re-evaluated. This is possible with the report ZVBRELB as described in note 78235.

9.4 Customer Specific Shelf Life Requirements

Without batch selection the 'minimum required shelf life date' is calculated as the confirmed date plus the required minimum shelf life as maintained in the product master.

The batch selection is an optional step and only necessary if customer specific required minimum shelf life exist or if the shelf life of the batches has to be checked for the deliveries. For the maintenance of a customer specific required shelf life value the class SHELF_LIFE_SEL of the type 023 for batches has to be created additionally as described in note 483576, figure 9.11.

Characteristic	Description	Data..	N..	D..	U..	Re..	Org. Areas
LOBM_RLZ	Remaining shelf life for batch	NUM	4	0	d	☑	
LOBM_LFDAT	Batch determin. delivery date	DATE	10	0		☐	
LOBM_VFDAT	Expiration date, shelf life	DATE	10	0		☐	

Fig. 9.11. Class SHELF_LIFE_SEL for the Calculation of the Required Shelf Life (R/3)

It is not required to assign the class to the material, nor must any of these characteristics be transferred to APO.

For the dependencies the function LOBM_UBD and the object dependencies LOBM_UBD have to be created as described in note 33396. The function is created with transaction CU65 and shown in figure 9.12:

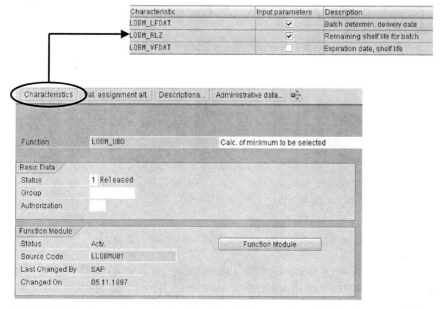

Fig. 9.12. Object Dependency for the Transfer of Customer Specific Requirements (R/3)

The object dependency itself is created with transaction CU01 and has to contain the coding as shown in figure 9.13.

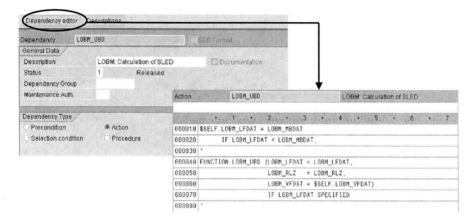

Fig. 9.13. Object Dependency LOBM_UBD (R/3)

For the assignment of the object dependency LOBM_UBD to the characteristic LOBM_RLZ it is necessary to execute the transaction BMSM. The result can be checked in transaction CT04 for the maintenance of characteristics, figure 9.14.

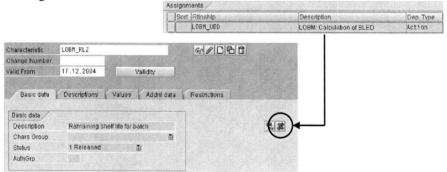

Fig. 9.14. Assignment of Object Dependency to Characteristic (R/3)

The search strategy is created for the strategy type SD01 with the key customer and material as described in chapter 5. The class SHELF_LIFE_SEL is assigned, figure 9.15.

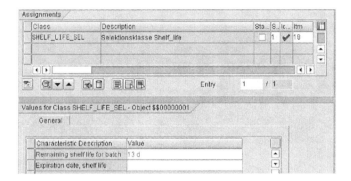

Fig. 9.15. Search Strategy for the Transfer of Customer Specific Requirements (R/3)

The value for the characteristic LOBM_RLZ (remaining shelf life for batch) represents the customer specific shelf life requirement. If the configuration is done correctly, the required minimum expiration date is calculated and stored in the sales order as shown in figure 9.16.

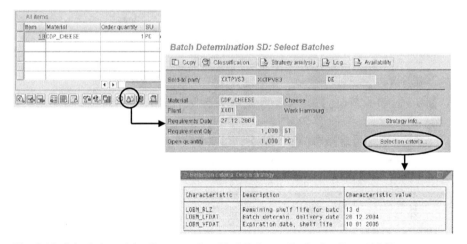

Fig. 9.16. Calculation of the Customer Specific Minimum Expiration Date (APO)

To transfer the required shelf life date to APO the user exit CIFSLS03 has to be activated (transaction SMOD) with the example coding as provided in note 483576, figure 9.17.

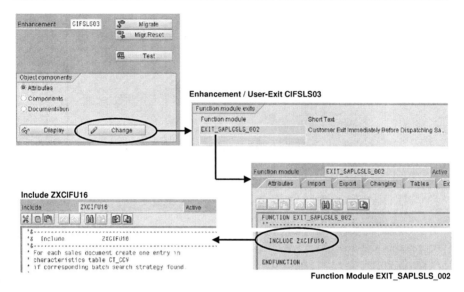

Fig. 9.17. User-Exit CIFSLS03 for the Transfer of the Required Shelf Life (R/3)

Additionally the user-exit has to be assigned to a customer project with transaction CMOD and the project has to be activated.

9.5 Production Planning and Scheduling with Shelf Life

Neither the sales order nor the forecast nor the planned or production orders have classes or characteristics assigned. Figure 9.18 shows the product view for a product with shelf life.

Avail/Rqmt	Avail/Re	Category	Receipt/Rqmt. Elemt	Rec/R	Confir.	Avail.	Surpl.	P.	C	N.	M.	Mty/Req. SLDate	ReqMaxSLDate
15.12.2004	00:00:00	Stock	0000000275/0002/CC	10	10	10	0						14.01.2005
15.12.2004	23:59:59		SNP Product Horizon										
17.12.2004	16:00:00	PrdOrd (C)	60003205	40	0	50	0	✓					16.01.2005
20.12.2004	00:00:00	FC req.	/1/6855	50-	0	0	0					30.12.2004	06.05.2032
20.12.2004	23:59:59	PlOrd. (F)	33221	10	0	10	5	✓					19.01.2005
26.12.2004	23:00:00	SalesOrder	10071/000010/1	5-	0	5	0					05.01.2005	13.05.2032
26.12.2004	23:00:00	SalesOrder	10071/000010/2	0	5-	5	0					05.01.2005	13.05.2032
03.02.2005	23:59:59		PP/DS Horizon										

CDP_CHEESE in XX01 (Make-to-stock)

Required Shelf Life of Requirement < Shelf Life of Receipt

Fig. 9.18. Product View for Shelf Life (APO)

Note that the indicator for 'planning with shelf life' triggers the inclusion of the columns 'minimum required shelf life date' and 'required maximum shelf life date' into the product view. The 'minimum required shelf life date' of the requirement has to be before the 'required maximum shelf life date' of the receipt to be shelf life compliant.

• *Production Planning*

Another impact of the shelf life design, since it is related to the pegging area (i.e. one locationproduct), is that shelf life is not propagated, if the locationproduct is processed in production or transported to another location. To consider the shelf life restrictions in production planning, the heuristic SAP_PP_SL001 has to be applied. This heuristic is a variant of the heuristic SAP_PP_002 as shown in figure 9.19.

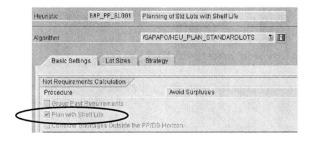

Fig. 9.19. Production Planning Heuristic SAP_PP_SL001 (APO)

Shelf life alerts are only calculated, if the flag for shelf life is set in the product master.

Though the SNP optimiser considers shelf life with some restrictions according to note 579556, its use is rather the exception. Since none of the other SNP functions support shelf life, it will be extremely difficult to interpret the result. The restriction that shelf life is limited to the location-product level remains for the SNP optimiser as well.

• *PP/DS Optimisation*

If the pegging relationship exists before calling the optimiser, the optimiser considers the pegging constraints. If no pegging exists, the optimiser ignores the shelf life constraints (i.e. the 'pegging' by the optimiser does not take shelf life into account).

9.6 Goods Receipt with Shelf Life Characteristics

At the goods receipt the production date has to be maintained to provide the shelf life information for the batch, figure 9.20.

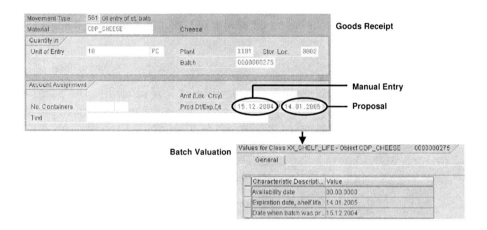

Fig. 9.20. Goods Receipt for Batches with Shelf Life (R/3)

The expiration date is calculated from the 'total shelf life'-value in the material master. This date is a proposal which can be overruled.

9.7 Shelf Life Alerts

To support the planning with shelf life there are specific alert types for shelf life within the PP/DS alert profile. Figure 9.21 shows these alert types.

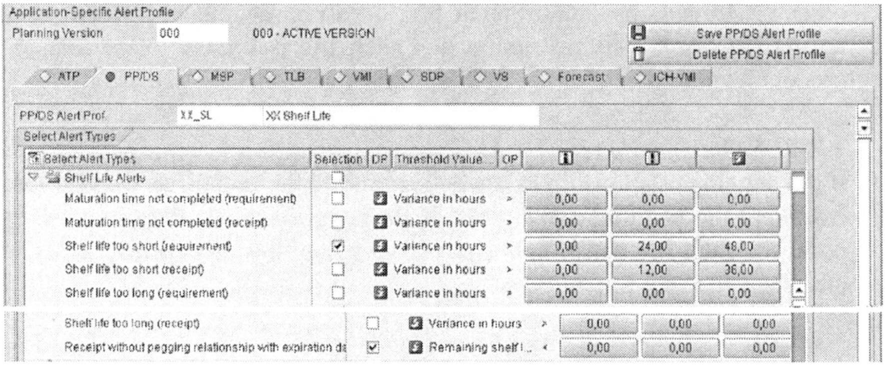

Fig. 9.21. Alert Profile for Shelf Life Planning (APO)

The alert types 'maturation time not completed', 'shelf life too short' and 'shelf life too long' indicate a violation of the pegging constraints. These kinds of violations are of course only possible when fix pegging is used. Depending whether requirements or receipts are chosen, the alert monitor will list the requirement or the receipt element. The alert type 'receipt without pegging relationship with expiration date' indicates that a receipt element is not pegged – probably due to incompatible shelf life properties. Figure 9.22 shows a planning situation and the resulting alerts.

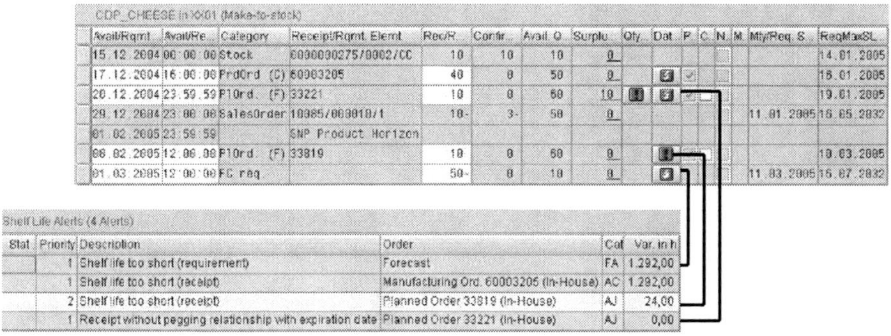

Fig. 9.22. Shelf Life Alerts (APO)

The flag for planning with shelf life in the product master is a prerequisite for the generation of shelf life alerts.

10 Sales Order Oriented Planning

10.1 Scenario Description

10.1.1 Process Chain

Many companies use neither a pure make-to-order nor a pure make-to-stock strategy but a mixture – either by using lot sizes for a make-to-order production or by planning for customers (with commitments to the customers) in a make-to-stock production. The idea of this scenario is to combine the advantage of the make-to-stock production (e.g. the consideration of inventories) with the planning without final assembly (production is only triggered if sales orders are available) and a requirements planning for individual customers.

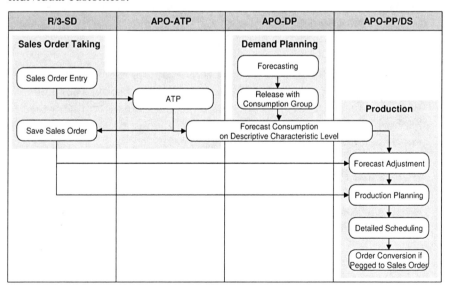

Fig. 10.1. Process Chain for Sales Order Oriented Planning

The scenario for sales order oriented planning contains three building blocks which differ from a typical make-to-stock scenario:

- Forecast consumption on customer or customer group level,
- adjustment of the forecast and the planned orders in the short term according to the sales order demand and
- planned order conversion depending on existing sales order requirements.

• Demand Planning and Forecast Consumption

Demand planning is performed on multiple levels – one of them is usually the customer or customer group level. The consumption of the forecast however does not take this level into account unless descriptive characteristics are used.

In many cases the forecast consumption on location and product level is sufficient or even desired because deviances can be levelled this way. The business assumption for using the forecast consumption on customer level is that if one customer exceeds the forecast, the other customers will still place sales orders for their planned demand.

• Sales Order Entry and ATP Check

For the use of descriptive characteristics in APO neither characteristics nor classes are required in R/3. Therefore no characteristic value assignment takes place during sales order taking. There are no functional restrictions for the ATP check in this scenario – a simple product check would be the most straightforward choice.

• Forecast Adjustment

In the short term horizon the forecast is reduced and the planned orders are adjusted as well in order not to block the resource capacity. The motivation for this step is the assumption that no more sales orders will be placed for this horizon. This is an optional step, and whether the assumption is appropriate or not depends on the individual case.

• Production Planning and Order Conversion

For production planning and detailed scheduling there are no peculiarities. The production – i.e. the planned order conversion into a production order – is however only triggered if the planned order is pegged to a sales order.

• Sales Order Oriented Planning for Make-to-Order

It is also possible to apply this process for a make-to-order strategy. This might be favourable if no pure make-to-order is used. An example for this is pharmaceutical production where the difference between many finished products lies mainly in the package and neither having inventory nor re-packaging of goods are an exception. The limitation for this process is that the ATP check is imprecise (checking horizon) or the result of the ATP check has to be corrected manually. The posting of goods from stock to the customer order assignment is an interactive process as well.

10.1.2 System Configuration Determinants

Sales order oriented planning relies on descriptive characteristics to ensure that the forecast for a customer or a customer group is not consumed by a different customer resp. customer group. For descriptive characteristics no class assignment is required – neither in R/3 nor in APO. Figure 10.2 shows the system configuration determinants.

Requirements Class Account Assignment	Class Type (R/3)	Configuration Scheme	Master Data
Make-to-Stock	Batch (023)	CDP	PPM
Make-to-Order	Variant Config. (300)	VC	PDS

Required / Supported
Supported but Unusual
Not Supported

Fig. 10.2. System Configuration Determinants for Sales Order Oriented Planning

The sales order oriented planning scenario is smoother for make-to-stock production, but as previously described it is also possible to apply this scenario for make-to-order with some restrictions.

No configuration relevance is required, but technically both types of configuration relevance might be used. For the same reason the use of the class types is indifferent to this scenario.

10.2 Descriptive Characteristics

The standard way of forecast consumption is on location and product level with the consequence that a more differentiated demand planning – for example on customer resp. customer group level or for different order types (e.g. express orders) – is undermined by an aggregated forecast consumption. With the use of descriptive characteristics it is possible to restrict the forecast consumption to location, product and descriptive characteristic.

The prerequisite for this functionality is the definition of a consumption group as described in chapter 4.2. No changes to the planning area or planning object structure are required, and no characteristics have to be assigned to the product master. The use of descriptive characteristics is entirely within APO, so no settings in R/3 are required. Note that only those characteristics can be used for this purpose that are used in the sales order as well.

• *Representation of the Forecast*
For each characteristic combination a separate forecast is created. This means that there are' more than one forecast orders for the same location-product at the same date. The descriptive characteristics use the ‚normal' characteristic functionality for the display – the green triangle. The details are displayed by double-clicking on this triangle.

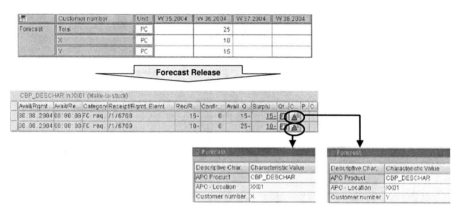

Fig. 10.3. Forecast with Descriptive Characteristics (APO)

In this example the forecast was performed on customer level.

• *Forecast Consumption*
The representation of the sales order in APO is similar as for the forecast – the green triangle exists, but the sales order contains only the descriptive characteristics as shown in figure 10.4.

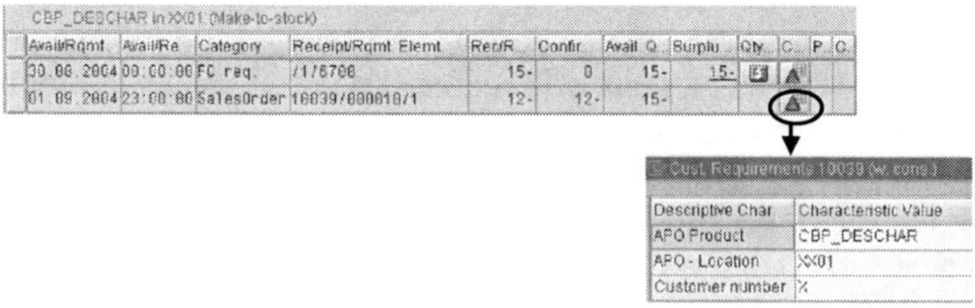

Fig. 10.4. Sales Order with Descriptive Characteristics (APO)

The forecast is consumed on the most detailed level, i.e. locationproduct and descriptive characteristic (in this case the customer). If the sales order for a characteristic value combination (here: customer X) exceeds the forecast quantity, the forecast for other characteristic value combinations (here: customer Y) is not consumed. A requirements strategy for planning with final assembly is used. Figure 10.5 displays the consumption situation (transaction /SAPAPO/DMP1) and shows that the values of the descriptive characteristics are taken into account.

Consumption Situation					
Date	To Date	Quantity...	Allocated	Rem. Pln...	Char./Value
30.08.2004	05.09.2004	10	10		Customer number/X
01.09.2004	01.09.2004				
30.08.2004	05.09.2004	15		15	Customer number/Y

Fig. 10.5. Forecast Consumption for Descriptive Characteristics (APO)

Using the 'characteristic/value' button it is possible to filter the forecast situation for certain characteristic values.

•Release Back to Demand Planning with Descriptive Characteristics
The release back to Demand Planning is used to provide the demand planner with an information about the feasibility of the demand plan. The information about the descriptive characteristic value is only available for the requirements (i.e. the forecasts and the sales orders) and not for the receipts. Using the pegging between the forecast and the planned order the according receipts are determined and transferred back to DP with the descriptive characteristic information. This is only possible for planned receipts and not for pegged stock elements.

10.3 Forecast Adjustment

The forecast is adjusted in order to have only sales orders as demands in the short-term. Two horizons are introduced for this:
- the ascertainment horizon, which is the basis for a detailed reporting of non-consumed forecast (in order to provide a help for manual intervention), and
- the adjustment horizon, in which the forecast is reduced by the adjustment heuristic. The planned orders are reduced accordingly.

The benefit of the forecast adjustment is that the capacity consumption on the resources is released and therefore the opportunity is given to improve the scheduling. This adjustment is only relevant for the short term and should only be applied if the assumption is valid that within this horizon usually no sales orders are placed.

The definition of the horizon for the ascertainment (i.e. reporting) and the adjustment is done in the product master in the PP/DS-view as shown in figure 10.6.

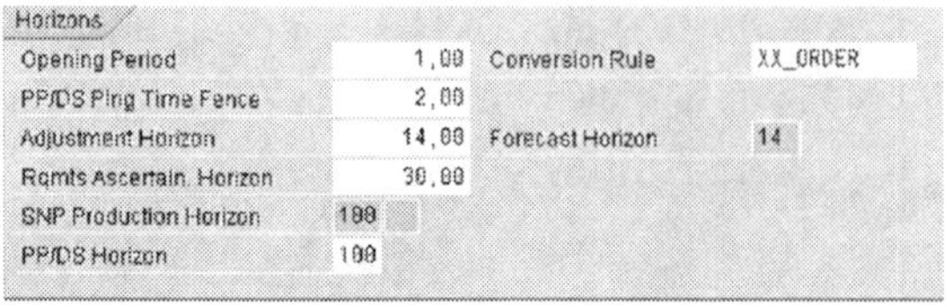

Horizons			
Opening Period	1,00	Conversion Rule	XX_ORDER
PP/DS Ping Time Fence	2,00		
Adjustment Horizon	14,00	Forecast Horizon	14
Rqmts Ascertain. Horizon	30,00		
SNP Production Horizon	100		
PP/DS Horizon	100		

Fig. 10.6. Settings in the Product Master for Ascertainment & Adjustment Horizons (APO)

We try to explain the significance of the ascertainment and the adjustment horizons with an example. Figure 10.7 shows the initial situation in the product view. The forecast is planned for the customers X and Y.

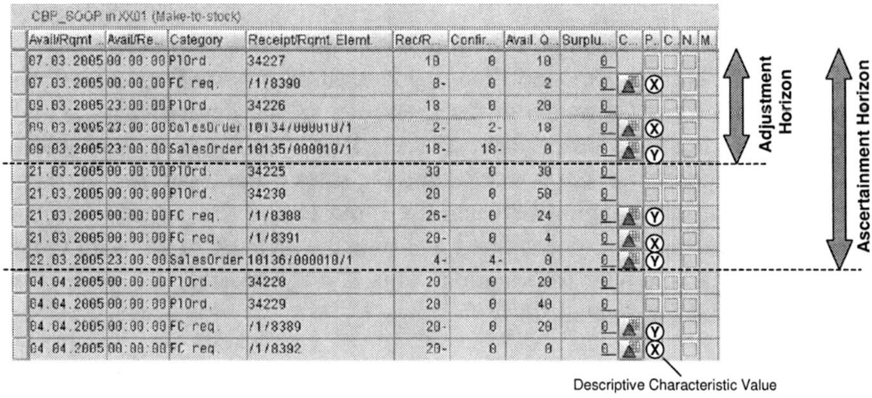

Fig. 10.7. Example for Sales Order Oriented Planning (APO)

In this example we have still forecast in the adjustment horizon. The values of the descriptive characteristics are displayed in the white circles. In contrast to the use of 'real' characteristics it is not possible to display the value of the descriptive characteristics as a separate column in the product view.

● *Ascertainment Horizon*

Since forecasting is performed on customer resp. customer group level and for each of these a different forecast element is created, it is more confusing to keep the overview about the consumption situation. Additionally aggregation usually levels the errors in forecasting and this is now missing. Therefore a report was developed to list the non-consumed forecast including the customer information within the ascertainment horizon as shown in figure 10.8

Product	Product Description	Location	QtyPlanned	Allocated	Rem PldQty	Reqmts Date	Rec/ReqQty	Total Qty	BUn	Characteristic/Value
CBP_SOOP	Sales Order Oriented Planning	XX01	30,000	4,000	26,000	21.03.2005	26-	30-	PC	Customer number Y
CBP_SOOP	Sales Order Oriented Planning	XX01	10,000	2,000	8,000	07.03.2005	8-	10-	PC	Customer number X
CBP_SOOP	Sales Order Oriented Planning	XX01	20,000	0,000	20,000	21.03.2005	20-	20-	PC	Customer number X

Fig. 10.8. Result of the Ascertainment Report (APO)

This report is included in the heuristic SAP_PP_014 and called via background production planning with the transaction /SAPAPO/CDPSB0.

• *Adjustment*
The adjustment heuristic SAP_PP_015 reduces the forecast and the planned orders within the adjustment horizon. Figure 10.9 shows the result of the adjustment heuristic based on the initial situation of figure 10.7.

Result Log of the Adjustment Heuristic

Statistic	Number
Orders selected	2
Adjustments of orders	1
Reorganization of Planned Ind. Reqmts	1
Orders with Errors	0

→ Adjustment of the Planned Order from 20 to 2
→ Reduction of the Forecast from 20 to 2
(2 are Consumed by Sales Order 10134)

CBP_SOOP in XX01 (Make-to-stock)

Avail/Rqmt...	Avail/Re...	Category	Receipt/Rqmt. Elemt.	Rec/R...	Confir...	Avail. Q...	Surplu...	C...	P...	C...	N...	M...
07.03.2005 02:00:00		PlOrd.	34227	2	0	2	0					
09.03.2005 23:00:00		PlOrd.	34226	18	0	20	0					
09.03.2005 23:00:00		SalesOrder	10134/000010/1	2-	2-	18	0					
09.03.2005 23:00:00		SalesOrder	10135/000010/1	18-	18-	0	0					

Fig. 10.9. Forecast Adjustment (APO)

The forecast is only reduced to its consumed value and not completely deleted.

10.4 Planned Order Conversion with Conversion Rules

The conversion rule is defined in customising with the path
> APO → *Supply Chain Planning* → *PP/DS* → *Transfer to Execution* →
> *Define Conversion Rule*.

and defines whether an ATP check and/or a requirements check is performed at the conversion of a planned order into a production order. The default conversion rule is defined in the global parameters and default values for PP/DS (transaction /SAPAPO/RRPCUST1) and optionally in the product master. The entry in the product master overrules the entry in the global parameters and default values, figure 10.10.

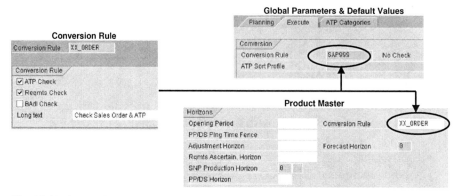

Fig. 10.10. Conversion Rule (APO)

The ATP check is performed in APO for the components of the planned order. The requirements check on the other hand looks at the pegging of the planned order and issues a warning if it is not pegged to a sales order. Depending whether the planned order quantity is partially pegged to a sales order or only pegged to forecast different warning messages pop-up for manual conversion:

Fig. 10.11. Warning for Conversion (APO)

If not the full quantity of the planned order is pegged – e.g. due to lot sizes – no warning is issued. The background conversion is not performed if a warning exists.

11 Production Planning and Scheduling

11.1 Production Planning with Characteristics

11.1.1 Production Planning with the VC-Configuration

The usage of the VC-configuration relevance is often linked with the use of object dependencies in R/3 and requires the PDS master data. For the products that are planned with the VC-configuration relevance, the characteristic values are not relevant for pegging. The connection between the requirement and the receipt is ensured by the sales order segment. Therefore variant configuration requires a make-to-order requirements strategy for a consistent process. The VC-configuration relevance does not have any impact on production planning. Figure 11.1 shows a planned order in APO for a product with the VC-configuration relevance.

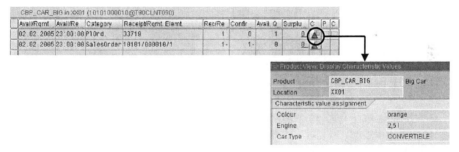

Fig. 11.1. Planned Order (VC-Configuration Relevance)

Though the planned order has characteristic values assigned, these are only a reference to the characteristic values of the sales order. It is possible to construct examples in R/3 with production orders that have an individual configuration of their own, but that is rather unusual.

11.1.2 Production Planning with the CDP-Configuration

With the CDP-configuration relevance the orders have valuations and requirements which contain the values of the characteristics. The valuations
in APO are integrated with the configuration in R/3 or the batch classification (for batches). The requirements in APO are integrated with the batch
selection criteria in R/3. Both the demand and the supply nodes (i.e. the
requirements and the receipts) of the locationproduct have valuations – or
at least they should. The valuations describe the value of the object itself
while the requirements of a demand represent the conditions for a receipt
to be pegged. If no supply with the same valuation exists, supplies with
matching valuations according to the requirements of the demand node are
considered. Only if no satisfactory supply exists, no pegging takes place.
This property is mainly used within the mill scenario for the assignment of
batches.

Figure 11.2 illustrates this behaviour for nominal characteristics. In case
3 where no matching supply exists a new receipt with the valuation of the
demand is created by production planning. The valuations of the demand
are used when a planned order is created in PP/DS.

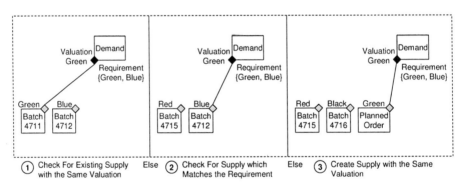

Fig. 11.2. Pegging for CDP-Configuration Relevance

Demands or supplies without a valuation resp. with incomplete requirements (unspecified characteristics) might cause problems in the further
course of the planning – especially if ATP on characteristics level is used.
A sub-optimal pegging is likely, in production planning an incorrect production plan might result and in the ATP overconfirmations might occur.
Note 526883 describes these risks in more detail.

Though pegging takes the CDP-configuration into consideration, the
pegging relations are not optimised – even if the configuration is complete
for all demands and supplies (see also note 526883). It might as well happen that demands are not covered though a different assignment of sup-

plies would allow this – and this might even happen to demands which have been covered before, as figure 11.3 shows. Net requirements calculation within production planning and pegging are separate steps with different rules.

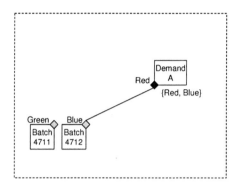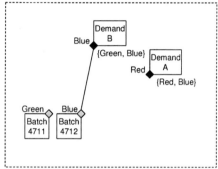

Fig. 11.3. Suboptimal Pegging and Stealing of Supplies

In this example two batches are available, one with the evaluation 'GREEN' and one with the evaluation 'BLUE'. The demand A has the requirement for 'RED' and 'BLUE', therefore the blue batch is pegged to the demand. Now a second demand B with the requirement for green and blue is created. Though it would be possible to cover both requirements if the green batch was pegged to demand B, a new pegging (which is triggered by the creation of a new demand node) might assign the blue batch to the new demand B with the consequence that demand A is not covered any more.

Up to APO 4.0 pegging arcs were only created if the valuation of the receipt element did match the requirements of the demand element. With APO 4.1 pegging takes place between identical valuations as well. Therefore the requirements are optional and should only be used if necessary.

● *Production Planning*
The standard production planning heuristics (e.g. SAP_PP_002) considers the CDP-configuration, therefore no change in the production planning is required. The valuation of the newly created planned order is the valuation of the demand node. If the demand node does not have any valuation (even if it does have requirements) the newly created planned order will not have any valuation either.

The performance requirements for production planning with CDP-configuration are much higher than without. This is a limitation for this process. Figure 11.4 shows a planned order in APO for the CDP-configuration relevance.

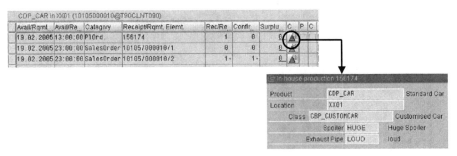

Fig. 11.4. Planned Order in APO (CDP-Configuration Relevance)

A rather substantial difference to the VC-configuration relevance is that planned orders are automatically converted into production orders when they are sent to R/3 if they have nodes with CDP-configuration relevance. The reason for this is that a planned order can not have a configuration of its own in R/3.

• *CDP in a Make-to-Stock Environment*
Differing from the VC-configuration relevance, production planning with CDP-configuration relevance can be used in a make-to-stock environment as well. In this case for the integration of the planned and production orders to R/3 the IS Mill solution is required however.

11.2 Detailed Scheduling with Characteristics

11.2.1 Impact of Characteristics on Detailed Scheduling

The characteristics information is either included in the pegging information (CDP-configuration and shelf life) or linked via customer order segments (VC-configuration). The impact of characteristics on scheduling has two aspects.

One is that scheduling considers the characteristics in the sense that scheduling is able to create results that are feasible in terms of matching configurations. The customer order assignment is always considered – i.e. it is not possible to assign receipts to requirements of different customer order segments. For the CDP-configuration relevance in a make-to-stock environment the pegging assignment between receipts and requirements might change if new demands or supplies are created or re-scheduled. The pegging in this case might be sub-optimal as described in this chapter earlier. The planning strategies within the scheduling heuristics control whether pegging and therefore the dependencies between receipts and requirements are considered.

The optimiser does consider customer order assignments and the CDP-configuration like the pegging does – independent of an existing pegging arc at the starting point. The shelf life constraints however are only considered if pegging already exists at the initial situation.

The other aspect of detailed scheduling with characteristics is how the characteristics are applied as a criterion for scheduling. In APO there are two different possibilities for that. One is to use the characteristic values as a sorting criterion for the scheduling sequence within the scheduling heuristics, the other is to reflect the different characteristic values by different set-up between the activities.

11.2.2 Characteristics as Sorting Criteria for Heuristics

The strategy profile and the scheduling heuristic SAP001 allow to define a sequence for scheduling both in interactive and in batch mode. For different criteria it is possible to define an ascending or a descending order – other sequences for sorting are not possible. If another sequence is required, a workaround using a different (new) field has to be used. Many common fields are available as sorting criteria but no characteristics since the characteristics are master data and implementation specific. It is however possible to define the characteristics as customer field and use them for sorting.

• *Characteristic Based Sequence Number*
The most convenient way to use characteristics values as sorting criteria is by setting the value of the 'sequence'-field in the operation via object dependencies as described in chapter 5.3.4. The reference characteristic has to influence the field SEQNR in APO. This field is part of the structure /SAPAPO/CULL_CFG_OPERATION.

• *Characteristics as Sorting Criteria for CDP-Configuration Relevance*
Another way to use characteristics to influence the sequencing in the scheduling heuristics is to make the characteristics available as sorting criteria. This is however only possible for the CDP-configuration relevance. The method GET_ORDDATA of the BAdI /SAPAPO/CDPS_ORDDATA has to be implemented and a field for the characteristics must be appended as customer field to the structure CI_ORDCUS. For this field the domain and

the data element have to be created. The structure CI_ORDCUS itself is part of another structure as shown in figure 11.5. All entries are on APO side.

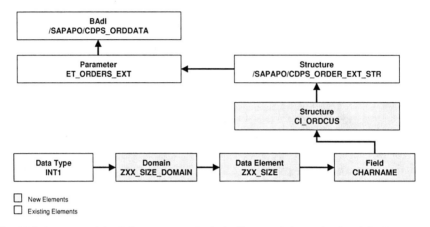

Fig. 11.5. Structure of the Enhancement to Include Characteristics as Sorting Criteria

Figure 11.5 shows an example where the characteristic CBP_SIZE is used as sorting criterion and the domain ZXX_SIZE_DOMAIN and the data element ZXX_SIZE have been created. The domain and the data element are created with the transaction SE11. The creation of the data element is explained in figure 11.6.

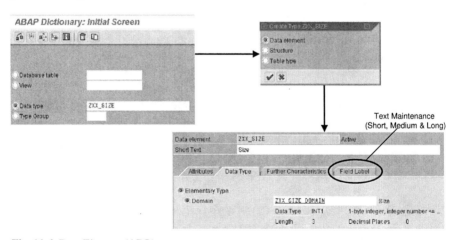

Fig. 11.6. Data Element (APO)

The field for the characteristic CBP_SIZE – in this case called CBP_SIZE as well – is assigned with the data element to the structure CI_ORDCUS. The structure is either created using the transaction SE11 or from the display of the top-level structure /SAPAPO/CDPS_ORDER_EXT_STR. In this example we defined the field CBP_SIZE in the structure CI_ORDCUS with the consequence that this field is available as a sorting criterion in the strategy (transaction /SAPAPO/CDPSC1) as shown in figure 11.7.

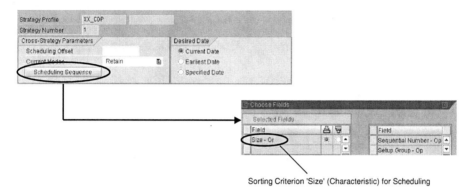

Sorting Criterion 'Size' (Characteristic) for Scheduling

Fig. 11.7. Characteristic as Sorting Criterion in the Strategy Profile (APO)

For display and performance reasons this characteristic should be included into the operation as well. The inclusion is done in the customising of the graphical objects in the planning board customising (transaction /SAPAPO/CDPSC2). Figure 11.8 shows the relevant steps to select the field for display.

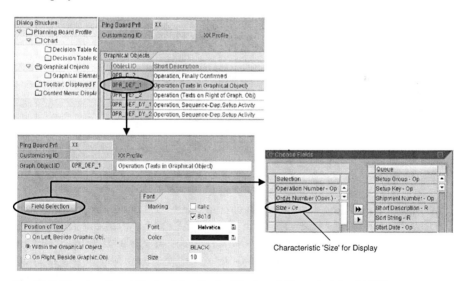

Characteristic 'Size' for Display

Fig. 11.8. Planning Board Customising for the Display of Characteristics (APO)

Finally the BAdI /SAPAPO/CDPS_ORDDATA has to be implemented in order to provide the planned order resp. production order with the characteristic value. An example for the usage of the characteristic CBP_SIZE (taken
from the output node of the order) is listed among the implementation
samples in the appendix.

11.2.3 Characteristics for Set-Up Group Determination

The use of sequence dependent set-up is a common way in APO to influence the sequence. As described in Dickersbach (2004), sequence dependent set-up is modelled in APO by assigning a set-up group resp. a set-up
key to the operation and defining the set-up duration between the set-up
groups resp. keys in a set-up matrix. One or more set-up keys are assigned
optionally to a set-up group to refine the set-up duration for certain set-up
groups. The set-up group or – if set-up keys are used - the set-up key is assigned to the PDS resp. the PPM on operation level. Though there is no
integration, the set-up group corresponds to the set-up group category in
R/3 and the set-up key to the set-up group key in R/3. The set-up matrix
defines the set-up duration between the set-up groups resp. the set-up keys
and is assigned to the resource as shown in figure 11.9.

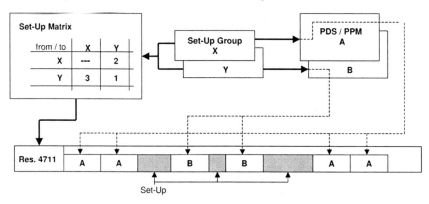

Fig. 11.9. Calculation of Sequence Dependent Set-Up (Dickersbach 2004)

Within the PPM the set-up group can be controlled depending on the value
of a characteristic as described in chapter 8.2. To control the set-up group
via object dependencies in the PDS it is necessary to use variant functions
because the set-up group is stored for the PDS as an internal key. Therefore a reference characteristic has to be used in APO and the value of the
reference characteristic (the internal key) has to be calculated via a function module as described in chapter 5.3.5. The structure for the set-up

group and the set-up key in the PDS is /SAPAPO/CULL_CFG_ACT_ALL, the fields are GROUP_ID for the set-up group and ITEM_ID for the set-up key.

• *Example How to Control the Set-Up Group with Object Dependencies*
In the following we describe an example how to control the set-up group based on the value of the characteristic CBP_COLOUR. The reference characteristic is XREF_ROUTINGSETUP, the variant function and the function module are ZXX_SETUP. The use of variant functions is defined in chapter 5 (e.g. in figure 5.20). The object dependency has to call the variant function ZXX_SETUP:

```
FUNCTION ZXX_SETUP
   (CBP_COLOUR = $ROOT.CBP_ COLOUR,
    XREF_ROUTINGSETUP = $SELF.XREF_ROUTINGSETUP)
```

The dependency group SAPAPOACT has to be assigned to the object dependency, and the object dependency has to be assigned to the operation of the routing. The function module ZXX_SETUP and the variant function ZXX_SETUP need to be created in APO as described in chapter 5.3.5. An example coding for the function module is listed as an implementation sample in the appendix.

To enable the sequence dependent set-up calculation the flag for sequence dependent set-up has to be set. This is done per default during the transfer of the PDS if the set-up group is set in the routing in R/3. If no set-up group is maintained in the routing, the relevance for sequence dependent set-up must be set explicitly via a reference characteristic in APO. The field that has to be referenced for this case is IS_SETUP_ACT of the structure /SAPAPO/CULL_CFG_ACT_SETUP.

11.3 Planned Order Integration

For the VC-configuration relevance the configuration of the planned order exists only as a reference to the configuration of the sales order, whereas a planned order with CDP-configuration relevance contains its own configuration without reference to the sales order. However, in the case of a product with CDP-configuration relevance and a make-to-order strategy the planned order references the sales order (in order to avoid inconsistencies at the integration with R/3).

In R/3 the planned order may only have configuration as a reference to the sales order, therefore only planned orders with VC-configuration relevance characteristics are transferred to R/3 as planned orders. If the planned order contains CDP-configuration relevance (at the output node), the planned order is automatically converted into a production order when transferred to R/3. Figure 11.10 shows the configuration of a planned order in R/3 that was transferred from APO (using the VC-configuration relevance).

Fig. 11.10. Planned Order in R/3 (VC-Configuration Relevance in APO)

The production order in R/3 is configurable – 11.11 shows the valuation of the production order.

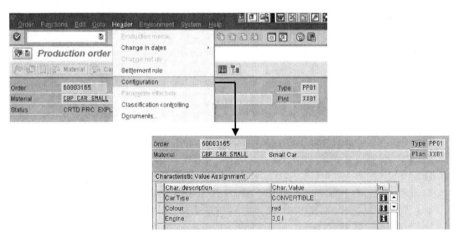

Fig. 11.11. Production Order in R/3

It does not make a difference for the production order whether the VC- or the CDP-configuration relevance is used in APO.

11.4 Display of Characteristics in the Product View

It is possible to display the characteristic values in the product view using the characteristic visualisation profile. The characteristic visualisation profile is defined with the customising path
> *APO* → *Supply Chain Planning* → *PP/DS* → *Product Planning Table* → *Define Visualisation Profiles.*

As shown in figure 11.12.

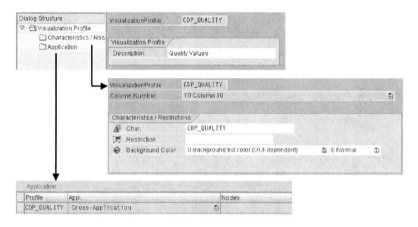

Fig. 11.12. Characteristic Visualisation Profile (APO)

The values of up to ten characteristics can be displayed this way (the characteristics are assigned to the visualisation profile and column number). The characteristic visualisation profile is assigned to the 'orders' view of the user settings as shown in figure 11.13.

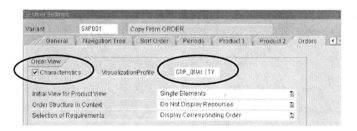

Fig. 11.13. Assignment of the Visualisation Profile to the User Settings (APO)

The result of this assignment is that a new column is created with the characteristic value as shown in figure 11.14.

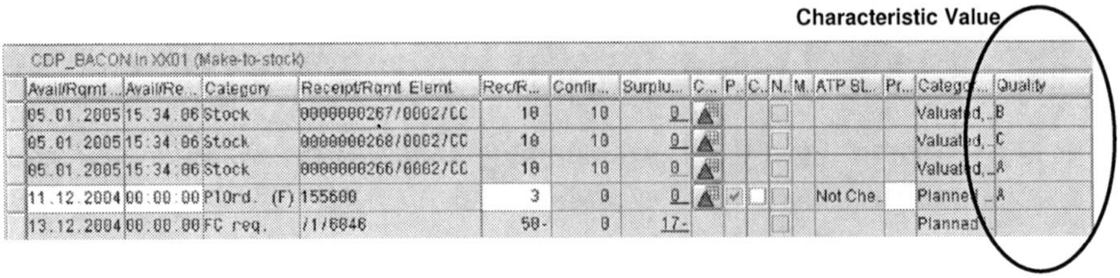

Characteristic Value

CDP_BACON in XX01 (Make-to-stock)														
Avail/Rqmt	Avail/Re	Category	Receipt/Rqmt Elemt	Rec/R	Confir	Surplu	C	P	C	N	M	ATP SL	Pr	Catego	Quality
05.01.2005 15:34:06	Stock	0000000267/0002/CC	10	10	0	▲							Valuated	B
05.01.2005 15:34:06	Stock	0000000268/0002/CC	10	10	0	▲							Valuated	C
05.01.2005 15:34:06	Stock	0000000266/0002/CC	10	10	0	▲							Valuated	A
11.12.2004 00:00:00	PlOrd. (F)	155600	3	0	0	▲	✓					Not Che.	Planne	A
13.12.2004 00:00:00	FC req.	/1/6846	50-	0	17-								Planned	

Fig. 11.14. Product View with the Display of Characteristic Values (APO)

This is a convenient way to provide an overview about the characteristic values of different orders.

For the CDP-configuration relevance it is additionally possible to filter orders via characteristics when entering the product view or within the product view using the triangle in the icon bar.

References

Literature

Dickersbach, J. Th.:
Supply Chain Management with APO.
Springer-Verlag, Berlin Heidelberg 2004

Eversheim, W.:
Organisation in der Produktionstechnik Band 1.
VDI-Verlag, Düsseldorf 1996

Knolmayer, G., Mertens, P., Zeier, A.:
Supply Chain Management Based on SAP Systems.
Springer-Verlag, Berlin Heidelberg 2002

OSS Notes

33396   Batch determination.: Selection with remaining life LOBM_RLZ

78235   Revaluating reference characteristics in batch classification

391018   Shelf life R/3 → APO, settings in R/3

426563   CTP: Settings, system behaviour and performance

453921   X: char. value, batch no., copy acc. assignment to RBATP item

483576   Required shelf life per customer/material without configuration

484144   Information on characteristics-based forecasting

495825   CDP definitions for block planning via user exit

526883   CDP: Unspecified characteristics in planning and pegging

528189   Additional information on block planning

551124   APO: Finite scheduling with MRP heuristic

601255   Variant functions cannot be created

602174   Standard LOBM_APO_SL* characteristics do not exist in client

604757   Incorrect variant functions and object dependencies

614280   Variant tables cannot be created

714929   Changing characteristic and class master data for CDP

751392   Shelf life R/3 → APO, settings in R/3 system

815018   Change of component using dependency

Abbreviations

APO	Advanced Planner and Optimiser
ATP	Available-to-Promise
BAdI	Business Add-In
BOM	Bill of Material
CBF	Characteristic Based Forecasting
CBP	Characteristic Based Planning
CDP	Characteristic Dependent Planning
CIF	Core Interface
CTM	Capable-to-Match
CTP	Capable-to-Promise
CVC	Characteristic Value Combination
DP	Demand Planning
GR	Goods Receipt
IS	Industry Solution
MLATP	Multi-Level ATP
MTO	Make-to-Order
MTS	Make-to-Stock
PDS	Production Data Structure
PIR	Planned Independent Requirement
PP/DS	Production Planning and Detailed Scheduling
PPM	Production Process Model
RBATP	Rules-Based ATP
RTO	Run-Time Object
SCM	Supply Chain Management
SNP	Supply Network Planning
TP/VS	Transportation Planning and Vehicle Scheduling
VC	Variant Configuration

Implementation Samples

For the detailed description about how to implement a function at several points in the book coding was required – either as object dependency, as BAdI or as a function module. In chapter 11.2 a BAdI and a function module are mentioned which require a more extensive coding. Examples for this coding are listed in this chapter.

• *BADI to Include Characteristics as Sorting Criteria*
As mentioned in chapter 11.2.2 it is possible to include characteristics as sorting criteria into the scheduling strategy and into the scheduling heuristic using the BAdI /SAPAPO/CDPS_ORDDATA. An example for the usage of the characteristic CBP_SIZE (taken from the output node of the order) is listed here:

```
method /SAPAPO/IF_EX_CDPS_ORDDATA~GET_ORDDATA.

  DATA: lv_charact_id        TYPE /sapapo/mc01ch_id,
        ls_gen_params        TYPE /sapapo/om_gen_params,
        lv_simsession        TYPE /sapapo/om_simsession,
        ls_exclude_exports   TYPE /sapapo/om_getdata_options,
        lt_orders            TYPE /sapapo/om_ordid_tab,
        lt_outputs           TYPE /sapapo/om_io_tab,
        lt_val               TYPE /sapapo/om_charact_val_tab,
        lt_rc                TYPE /sapapo/om_lc_rc_tab.

  FIELD-SYMBOLS: <ls_order>   LIKE LINE OF it_orders,
                 <ls_output>  LIKE LINE OF it_outputs,
                 <ls_ord_ext> LIKE LINE OF et_orders_ext,
                 <ls_val>     LIKE LINE OF lt_val.

* get internal ID of characteristic:
  CALL METHOD /sapapo/cl_mc01_ccv_struct=>charname_as_id
    EXPORTING
      ic_charname = 'CBP_SIZE'
    IMPORTING
      en_charid   = lv_charact_id
    EXCEPTIONS
      OTHERS      = 2.
  CHECK sy-subrc IS INITIAL.
```

```
   LOOP AT it_orders
       ASSIGNING <ls_order>.
     APPEND <ls_order>-orderid
         TO lt_orders.
   ENDLOOP. " AT it_orders
   SORT lt_orders.
   DELETE ADJACENT DUPLICATES
     FROM  lt_orders.

* get charact. data of order output nodes from liveCache:
   CALL FUNCTION '/SAPAPO/RRP_SIMSESSION_GET'
      IMPORTING
        ev_simsession = lv_simsession
        es_gen_params = ls_gen_params.
   CLEAR ls_exclude_exports WITH 'X'.
   CLEAR:  ls_exclude_exports-get_charact_outnode.

   CALL FUNCTION '/SAPAPO/OM_ORDER_GET_DATA'
      EXPORTING
        is_gen_params               = ls_gen_params
        iv_simsession               = lv_simsession
        it_order                    = lt_orders[]
        is_exclude_exports          = ls_exclude_exports
      IMPORTING
*       et_charact_val_acts         =
*       et_charact_req_inpnode      =
        et_charact_val_outnode      = lt_val[]
        et_rc                       = lt_rc[]
      EXCEPTIONS
        lc_connect_failed           = 1
        lc_com_error                = 2
        lc_appl_error               = 3.
   CHECK sy-subrc IS INITIAL.
   SORT  lt_val
     BY  object_id
         object_type
         position_no
         line_no
         charact_id.

* provide sorting value for orders from characteristics:
   SORT  lt_outputs
     BY  orderid
         position_no
         line_no.
   LOOP AT et_orders_ext
       ASSIGNING  <ls_ord_ext>.
*    get output for order (assuming only 1 output):
     READ TABLE it_outputs
       ASSIGNING  <ls_output>
       WITH KEY  orderid = <ls_ord_ext>-ordid
       BINARY SEARCH.
```

```
      CHECK sy-subrc IS INITIAL.

*     get characteristic value for output:
      READ TABLE lt_val
        ASSIGNING  <ls_val>
        WITH KEY
          object_id   = <ls_output>-orderid
          position_no = <ls_output>-position_no
          line_no     = <ls_output>-line_no
          charact_id  = lv_charact_id.
      CHECK sy-subrc IS INITIAL.
      <ls_ord_ext>-CBP_SIZE = <ls_val>-quan_value.
    ENDLOOP. " AT et_orders_ext

endmethod.
```

Special cases as by-products are ignored in this example.

• *Function Module to Determine the Set-Up Group Identifier*
Not all fields have a simple correspondence between R/3 and APO. For the
use of reference characteristics this implies that variant functions might be
required to determine the APO internal identifiers for some fields. An example coding for the function module (called by the variant function) to
determine the identifier for the set-up group is listed in the following as
mentioned in chapter 11.2.3. In this case the set-up group is set to 'XX2' if
the value of CBP_COLOUR is 'RED'.

```
FUNCTION ZXX_SETUP.
*"----------------------------------------------------------
*"*"Local Interface:
*"  IMPORTING
*"     REFERENCE(GLOBALS) LIKE  CUOV_00 STRUCTURE  CUOV_00
*"  TABLES
*"     QUERY STRUCTURE   CUOV_01
*"     MATCH STRUCTURE   CUOV_01
*"  EXCEPTIONS
*"     FAIL
*"     INTERNAL_ERROR
*"----------------------------------------------------------

  data:
    lv_apo_group_id TYPE  /SAPAPO/CDPS_SETUP_ID,
    lv_apo_ITEM_ID  TYPE  /SAPAPO/CDPS_SETUP_ID,
    lv_SETUP_GROUP  TYPE  /SAPAPO/CDPS_SETUP_GROUP,
    lv_SETUP_ITEM   TYPE  /SAPAPO/CDPS_SETUP_ITEM,
    ls_CUOV_01      TYPE  CUOV_01,
    lv_SETUP_ID     TYPE  /SAPAPO/CDPS_SETUP_ID.
```

```
READ TABLE QUERY
  WITH KEY VARNAM = 'CBP_COLOUR'
  INTO ls_CUOV_01.

CHECK sy-subrc = 0.

IF ls_CUOV_01-atwrt = 'RED'.
  lv_SETUP_GROUP = 'XX2'.
ENDIF.

CALL FUNCTION '/SAPAPO/DM_SETUP_ID_READ'
  EXPORTING
    i_locid       = 'LjGhTBmHSKQa3r65jIOOyW'
    i_setup_group = lv_setup_group
    i_setup_item  = lv_setup_item
  IMPORTING
    e_setup_id    = lv_setup_id
  EXCEPTIONS
    not_found     = 1
    OTHERS        = 2.

CALL FUNCTION '/SAPAPO/DM_SETUP_IDS_GET'
  EXPORTING
    i_setup_id        = lv_setup_id
  IMPORTING
    e_setup_group_id  = lv_apo_group_id
    e_setup_item_id   = lv_apo_item_id
  EXCEPTIONS
    not_found         = 1
    OTHERS            = 2.

CLEAR ls_CUOV_01.
ls_CUOV_01-varnam = 'XREF_ROUTINGSETUP_GROUP'.
ls_CUOV_01-atflv  = lv_apo_group_id.
ls_CUOV_01-atfor  = 'NUM'.

APPEND ls_CUOV_01 to MATCH.

ENDFUNCTION.
```

Since the internal key for the set-up group is location dependent, the function /SAPAPO/DM_SETUP_ID_READ needs the GUID of the location as an input. The GUID is stored in the table /SAPAPO/LOC.

Transactions

For the quick access of some functions this chapter provides a list of useful transactions for planning with characteristics. Most of these have been explained in the text.

Characteristics and Classes

System	Description of the Transaction	Transaction
R/3, APO	Characteristics	CT04
R/3, APO	Class	CL02
R/3, APO	Assignment of Class to Product	CL24N
R/3, APO	Organisational Area	O1CL

Variant Configuration

System	Description of the Transaction	Transaction
R/3	Configuration Profile	CU41
R/3	Object Dependency	CU01
R/3	Object Dependencies Check	CU50
APO	PDS Display & Config. Simulation	/SAPAPO/CURTO_SIMU
R/3, APO	Variant Functions	CU65
R/3	BOM Assignment to Material Variant	CS40
R/3	Routing Assignment to Mat. Variant	CA02
R/3, APO	Variant Table – Definition	CU61
R/3, APO	Variant Table – Data Maintenance	CU60

Batch Selection and ATP with Characteristics

System	Description of the Transaction	Transaction
R/3	Batch Selection Search Strategy	VCH1
R/3	Batch Customising	OCHA
R/3	Sort Sequence for Characteristics	CU70
APO	Rules	/SAPAPO/RBA04
APO	Characteristic View (ATP)	/SAPAPO/ATPCH01

Characteristic Based Forecasting

System	Description of the Transaction	Transaction
APO	CBF- Profile Maintenance	/SAPAPO/IPM01
APO	CBF- Profile Maintenance (old)	/SAPAPO/DPC1
APO	Characteristic Value Combinations	/SAPAPO/MC62
APO	Consumption Group	/SAPAPO/CSP1
APO	Forecast Release	/SAPAPO/MC90
APO	Forecast Reorganisation	/SAPAPO/MD74
APO	Transform. of Dependent Demand	/SAPAPO/DMP2
APO	Consumption Overview	/SAPAPO/DMP1

Block Planning

System	Description of the Transaction	Transaction
APO	Resource	/SAPAPO/RES01
APO	PPM	/SAPAPO/SCC05
APO	Forecast Generation from Blocks	/SAPAPO/BLRG01

Shelf Life

System	Description of the Transaction	Transaction
R/3	Update Shelf-Life Characteristics	BMSM

Production Planning and Detailed Scheduling

System	Description of the Transaction	Transaction
APO	Product View	/SAPAPO/RRP3
APO	Pegging Overview	/SAPAPO/PEG1
APO	Global Parameters and Default Values	/SAPAPO/RRPCUST1
APO	Background Planning	/SAPAPO/CDPSB0
APO	Scheduling Strategy Profile	/SAPAPO/CDPSC1
APO	Planning Board Customising	/SAPAPO/CDPSC2
APO	PP/DS Heuristics	/SAPAPO/CDPSC11

Index

Printing and Binding: Strauss GmbH, Mörlenbach

CPSIA information can be obtained at www.ICGtesting.com
Printed in the USA
LVOW082115081012

302056LV00005B/17/P